"What makes friendship *good*? How can we enlarge our care for one another? As a skilled physician of the soul, Brad Hambrick combines his rich understanding of Scripture with his genuine curiosity about people and then beautifully articulates this doctrine of transformational friendship. Leave it to Brad to carefully and methodically communicate a message that the body of Christ is so desperate to hear."

Ann Maree Goudzwaard, Executive Director, Help[H]er

"In a world of inch-deep and mile-wide relationships, there seems to be a gap between people's desire for rich friendships and the lack of depth in their current relationships. This book is not only a gospel-saturated reflection of that pursuit but a tangible roadmap for helping you get there. A timely resource that I think all church leaders should have on their shelves."

Jason Gaston, Executive Pastor of Next Gen, Biltmore Church, Arden, NC

"Living in a time when loneliness and isolation are reaching epidemic proportions, *Transformative Friendships* tells a better story and points to a better way. Offering rich insights aimed at building lasting friendships, Brad Hambrick winsomely hands the reader seven simple and meaningful questions to ask that will undoubtedly deepen any relationship. This book is immensely practical and desperately needed."

Will Toburen, Lead Pastor, Calvary Baptist Church, Winston-Salem, NC

"Here in his latest work, Brad Hambrick encourages us to build simple and meaningful friendships in a way that feels neither programmed nor painful. He offers a simple framework of questions that can be extrapolated in a million different ways but ultimately leads you toward a deeper, richer sense of knowing one another. I'm thrilled that what I get to experience regularly in my friendship with Brad is now yours to share through this enriching and engaging book."

Jonathan Holmes, Executive Director, Fieldstone Counseling

"What Brad offers to us in these pages is a timeless framework for nourishing personal relationships. If you're looking for a practical guide for cultivating friendships with wisdom and intention, this helpful book is it!"

Christine M. Chappell, Author of *Midnight Mercies: Walking with God through Depression in Motherhood*; *Hope + Help Podcast* host, Institute of Biblical Counseling & Discipleship; certified biblical counselor

"In a trying time, pastors and counselors cannot walk as closely with you as a true friend can. That's why *Transformative Friendships* is such a necessary resource for believers today. Regular engagement in Brad Hambrick's seven questions will produce depth in any relationship and build a foundation for friendships that traverse every season of life."

David Talbert, Small Groups Pastor, The Summit Church, Durham, NC

TRANSFORMATIVE FRIENDSHIPS

7 QUESTIONS TO DEEPEN ANY RELATIONSHIP

Brad Hambrick

New Growth Press, Greensboro, NC 27401
newgrowthpress.com

Cover Design: Faceout Books, faceoutstudio.com
Interior Typesetting and eBook: Lisa Parnell, lparnellbookservices.com

ISBN: 978-1-64507-333-8 (Print)
ISBN: 978-1-64507-334-5 (eBook)

Library of Congress Cataloging-in-Publication Data

Names: Hambrick, Brad, 1977– author.
Title: Transformative friendships : 7 questions to deepen any relationship / Brad Hambrick.
Description: Greensboro, NC : New Growth Press, [2024] | Series: Church-based counseling | Includes bibliographical references. | Summary: "Shares seven simple questions that will help you be intentional about deepening and strengthening friendships that will enrich your life"— Provided by publisher.
Identifiers: LCCN 2023038921 (print) | LCCN 2023038922 (ebook) | ISBN 9781645073338 (print) | ISBN 9781645073345 (ebook)
Subjects: LCSH: Friendship—Religious aspects—Christianity.
Classification: LCC BV4647.F7 H353 2024 (print) | LCC BV4647.F7 (ebook) | DDC 241/.6762—dc23/eng/20231122
LC record available at https://lccn.loc.gov/2023038921
LC ebook record available at https://lccn.loc.gov/2023038922

Printed in the USA

31 30 29 28 27 26 25 24   1 2 3 4 5

CONTENTS

Contents

Introduction:
SIMPLE YET POWERFUL

Friendship is simple and meaningful. And that is how a book on friendship should be written. As you read this book, I hope your consistent response is, "That's not hard. Maybe a little more vulnerable than I'd prefer, but I could do that. Yeah, I think my life would be better if my friendships were more like that." Page after page, that's what we're after: simple and meaningful.

But don't mistake simplicity for weakness. Many simple things have (or would have) a powerful impact on our lives: a daily time of reading the Bible and praying, consistently having a family meal together, and getting adequate sleep each night. None of these things is complicated, but each is powerful. Being and having a good friend belongs on the list. It's a simple thing that has a life-changing impact. That is what we will cultivate in the pages ahead.

But it's not just friendship itself that's simple yet powerful. *How* we cultivate friendship is simple and powerful too. That's why, in our journey together, we will use seven simple questions.

1. What's your story?
2. What's good?
3. What's hard?
4. What's bad?
5. What's fun?
6. What's stuck?
7. What's next?

Hopefully, it's not intimidating to imagine yourself asking a friend these questions, or being asked them by a friend. In the pages that follow, we'll unpack how these simple questions can transform casual acquaintances into "iron sharpens iron" (Proverbs 27:17) friendships that become dearer than family: "There is a friend who sticks closer than a brother" (Proverbs 18:24).

Imagine what it would be like if the people closest to you engaged with you in these meaningful ways. That is what God designed the church to be—a place of *belonging*, not just *learning*. Christian education is wonderful, but God didn't create churches to be micro-seminaries. God created churches to be places of mutual care within deepening relationships; hence, family is a dominant metaphor for the church.

With that in mind, you will be invited to *practice* your way through this book, not merely *read*. The reality is, you don't grow deeper friendships merely by gaining a clearer understanding of what friendship "ought" to be. You grow in friendship by engaging with your existing friends in more meaningful ways. So, as you move through each of these seven questions, you should have two questions in mind:

1. Where are my existing friendships?
2. What would be "next" in deepening my existing friendships?

From there, you look for the next opportunity to ask a more meaningful question, engage in an activity together, or share a new part of your story. This book is filled with questions, activities, and prompts to deepen your relationships. Find where you are and take the next step!

But some of us come to this book dry and skeptical. We've wanted meaningful friendships for a long time and haven't been able to cultivate them. If that's you, what makes you say, "Yeah, but . . ."? Don't be afraid to speak it. Your apprehensions are welcome on this journey. Friendship is never fake.

Yet here is a challenge for you: *doubt your fears about friendship*. Doubt those fears enough to leave room for the possibility that the friendships you long for are possible. Most of us brace against being disappointed: "Hope deferred makes the heart sick" (Proverbs 13:12). That's common. But don't allow the fear of disappointment to result in passivity that becomes a self-fulfilling prophecy.

If we were trying to build a set of perfect friendships, fear would be warranted. We *would* be disappointed. But our goal is more modest. We simply want to incrementally deepen our existing relationships so that they have more of the redemptive influence God intended friendships to have. Good friendships cook in a Crock-Pot, not a microwave.

That's our goal: *simple questions producing friendships that enrich our lives a little more each day*.

GROWING DEEPER ROOTS

Every project needs a plan. Every journey needs a map. For this one, we will use a picture metaphor: a tree with growing roots. Our goal with each of the seven simple questions will be to grow deeper in our friendships. We will start at depth one and work our way to depth five, using the picture of the tree and its roots to show how deep we are going as we explore that question.

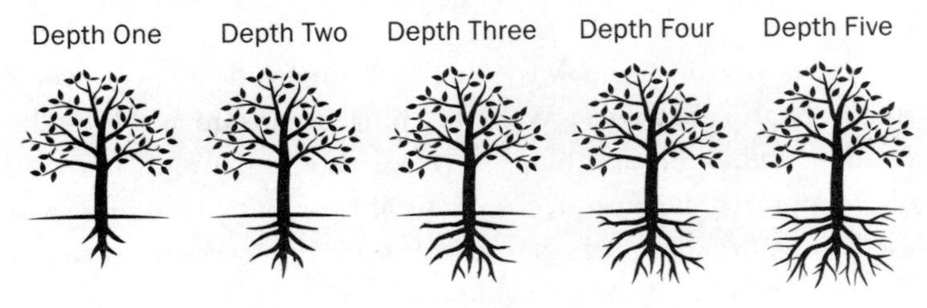

Here's the advantage of this approach: it starts where each friendship is. Sometimes, when Christians talk about things like friendship, we focus so much on the ideal that it's overwhelming. It feels too far off to be achieved. By contrast, we'll focus on growth rather than the destination.

For each of our seven questions, we will follow a predictable pattern. First, we will **define why each question is important**. What is the good thing this question cultivates within a friendship? How does it nudge the roots deeper?

Second, we will **identify the five depths of growth** for each question. Early depths are achievable for casual friendships. Enjoy these early depths. Don't rush them. But do begin moving some of your friendships to greater depths that can have a more meaningful impact on your life. We'll explore questions to ask and the kinds of things you might share to reach each depth of friendship.

Finally, in each section, we will **conclude with a summative exercise**. This is a way to solidify the work done on that question and make it a permanent part of your friendship culture.

We could summarize this in three simple phrases:

1. Know what you're pursuing.
2. Know the little wins on the way to the big win.
3. Know how to cement the growth you've achieved.

As you prepare for this journey, I encourage you to think in terms of *rhythms*, *habits*, and *lifestyles* more than *tasks*, *objectives*, and *protocols*. The latter tend to be well-intended but short-lived. The former are the things that shape extended seasons of our lives.

Ironically, if this book is going to change your life, you won't think about it that often. We're teaching friendship as a lifestyle, not as a skill. Skills are things we focus on and master. Lifestyles, once embraced, begin to feel so natural we don't pay attention to them anymore. Friendships that transform our lives are rooted in simple things we naturally do hundreds of times.

Hopefully, this prompts you to breathe a sigh of relief. We're not aiming for perfect friendships concocted quickly with complex skills. We're cultivating deep friendships that grow steadily over time through simple questions and common interactions. We're not setting aside a season of our life to go to friendship boot camp.

We're just going to intentionally invest in our current friendships within our existing rhythms of life.

HOW MANY THIRTY-FIVES SHOULD I HAVE?

I know some of you. You saw a list of seven questions, and you saw there are five levels of depth for each, and you started doing math. You realized that a perfect friendship score is thirty-five. You immediately concluded, "I want a life full of depth-thirty-five friendships, and Brad is going to show me the way!" It's okay. You can admit it.

Having a number like thirty-five allows us to address questions that may have been hard to articulate otherwise. How many "optimal" friendships should we strive for? Is it better to have one depth-thirty-five friend or several depth-twenty-five friends? Are depth-fifteen friendships of any real value or are they only "greenhouse" friendships that might grow into something worthwhile in time?

Anybody else having flashbacks to middle school? We're not asking these questions to compete in some artificial social hierarchy. That was middle school. It was miserable, and we don't want to go through it again. We're asking these questions to determine the preferred outcome for this book.

The answer is that *we don't want all depth-thirty-five friendships*. That's not realistic within the time constraints of life. We could make a pragmatic appeal and say that's just not how life works. But there is a stronger argument to be made. Variety in the topography of our friendships is good. More than this, the Bible affirms a variety in the depth and quality of friendships between Christians.

- Jesus had an inner circle of three friends, Peter, James, and John (Matthew 17:1; Luke 8:51) within his primary network of twelve disciples. But Jesus also casually connected with at least five hundred people (1 Corinthians 15:6).
- Paul had several people he was especially close with, like Timothy who was to him "as a son with a father" (Philippians 2:22). But Paul was close enough to many other people

> to mention them by name in his letters (see the long list in Romans 16:1–16).

The Bible doesn't call us to a perfect friendship standard. We shouldn't expect that either. The Bible affirms the beauty and value of friendships from depth five to thirty-five. We should too. BFFs aren't the ultimate goal. Casual acquaintances aren't starter relationships.

The Bible calls us to be agents of encouragement, salt, light, and mutual sharpening in each friendship as that relationship allows. This is what the "one another" commands of the New Testament describe: Christian friends enriching one another's lives at whatever depth their current friendship exists. A complete list of these "one another" passages is provided in this book's appendix and makes a great complement for your personal Bible reading as you read this book.

If we enrich other Christians, our churches will do more than theologically educate our minds, our workplaces will do more than provide financially for our families, and our gyms will do more than strengthen our bodies. Incrementally deepening our relationships in each of these spheres will start to transform our lives.

With seven simple questions and a dash of intentionality, we can experience friendships at depth five, ten, fifteen, twenty, twenty-five, thirty, and thirty-five that will enrich our lives. That's what we're after in this book. Don't get distracted by the big number thirty-five. Invest in and be content with what each of your friendships has to offer.

Allow Paul's words to his friend Timothy to shape how you approach this book: "But godliness with contentment is great gain" (1 Timothy 6:6). For this book, *godliness* will take the form of fulfilling the "one another" commands in our friendships of varying depth, and *contentment* will look like enjoying each friendship at its current depth. As we journey toward more meaningful friendships, let's bring together the rare combination of intentionality and contentment and see what God does.

Question One: What's Your Story?

Depth One: The Facts

Depth Two: The Major Themes

Depth Three: The Plot Twists

Depth Four: The Life-Shaping Events

Depth Five: The Point of Your Story

I grew up in a one-stoplight town. Everyone knew what you did on Saturday night by the time you rolled into church on Sunday morning. The doctor (yes, singular) in my town didn't take family histories because he didn't have to. That was the rest of his caseload. He knew everyone's story. Everyone knew everyone else's story, even three generations back.

Contrary to my early experience, the US Census Bureau has found that the average American will move eleven times over the course of their life.[1] Each time we move, we get to (have to) reinvent ourselves. No one in the new city knows us, knows our family, knows our successes, knows our failures, knows our quirks—knows our story. We begin writing our story on the blank canvas

---

1. "Calculating Migration Expectancy Using ACS Data," United States Census Bureau, updated December 3, 2021, https://www.census.gov/topics/population/migration/guidance/calculating-migration-expectancy.html.

of an entirely new social context. That is a peculiar combination of exciting, dangerous, and common.

It should startle us how few people really know our story. They know our social media feeds and public persona. They know a few sound bites from anecdotes we share together. But that's about it. No wonder we feel lonely, unknown, and relationally anemic.

When someone knows our story, we gain a sense of belonging. When people know our story, we can talk about personal experiences without explaining all the characters, contexts, and conflicts. People who know our story pick up on the ironies of our life. Being known creates a sense of freedom to talk and a confidence that we'll be understood. That is what we are cultivating as we share our stories more deeply.

We would like to think this kind of thing just happens. Sometimes it does. Sometimes we click with someone, sharing comes easy, and the relationship promptly gains depth. But most of us can attest that this doesn't happen frequently enough to be relied upon to cultivate meaningful community. Our cultural epidemic of loneliness, to which the church is not immune, is ample evidence of this.

That's why we'll explore a steady progression of getting to know someone's story and allowing our story to be known. We need to allow each friendship to develop at its own pace. Some will grow quickly, others gradually. This may be because of our season of life, available time, common interests, or other factors. But pace is not the most important concern.

Proportionality, however, is important. The modern proverb "Knowledge is power" is true. When one person knows much more about the other person, the relationship is imbalanced. A friendship inadvertently mutates into a helping relationship.

There is nothing wrong with helping relationships, like a teacher–student or counselor–counselee relationship. These can be very good relationships. But they are not what we are cultivating in this book. We are striving for balanced friendships of mutual care and mutual awareness.

When the Bible refers to one-another relationships, this language implies balance. This book is a tool to multiply and enrich these balanced friendships in your life and throughout your church. For a description of how to create more formal helping relationships within your church, consider reading this book's companion volume, *Mobilizing Church-Based Counseling*.[2]

This means you should pace your sharing by your friend's sharing. If you have disclosed more, be intentional about asking questions. If your friend is uncomfortable sharing more, allow the friendship to acclimate to its new depth. As life prompts more awareness between the two of you, continue to match the depth of disclosure you receive.

2. Brad Hambrick, *Mobilizing Church-Based Counseling: Models for Sustainable Church-Based Care* (Greensboro: New Growth Press, 2023). See particularly chapter 9.

Chapter 1
WHAT'S YOUR STORY? THE FACTS
DEPTH ONE

What is your favorite song that tells a life story? Perhaps it's "Butterfly Kisses" by Bob Carlisle, which traces the journey of a father and daughter from their earliest bedtime prayers to her sweet-sixteen birthday party to a final conversation before he walks her down the aisle on her wedding day. Where did the time go?

Maybe you've got a classic rock edge and you prefer "Cat's in the Cradle" by Harry Chapin. It's a less sanctified story of tables turning on a busy, big-city father who can't find time between business endeavors to play catch with his son. Then that son grows up to be just like dad and can't find time to squeeze in a meaningful phone call with his retired old man. How could the father be so blind?

You might be an 80s country fan who sings along with Garth Brooks's "Unanswered Prayers." This ballad revels in a Southern sweet tea theology reflecting on an encounter with an old high school flame at a small-town football game. Hindsight makes clear that some of God's most gracious answers to prayer are a simple no. What would I have missed?

These songs are examples of *what's your story* depth one in lyrical form. The experiences are so common: bedtime routines, young professionals trying to build a career while they raise children, or middle-aged adults shaking their heads at the prayers of their youth. It is almost as if they are singing about reheating leftovers on a Tuesday night.

But these songs impact us deeply—deeply enough to become timeless classics. We hear them and we cherish simple bedtime routines, we resolve to prioritize key relationships over opportunities, and we pray a little more humbly. We feel connected to these artists as they seemingly put our story to a melody.

What's our takeaway? These songs help us realize that the most significant parts of life are often the most common parts of life, that getting to know the common details of somebody's life is simple and powerful. The majority of what God wants to do in our life or our friend's life will be in those mundane moments and everyday relationships. Even if those moments aren't "exciting," the powerful influence of ordinary moments lived well makes them worth knowing.

What does this simple knowing look like? Be curious. Ask questions. Listen well. Remember names and special events. Follow up about key people or events. Smile at happy things. Reflect compassion for sad things. Again, we see that being a friend is not complicated, but its impact is profound.

Consider Luke 12:7 where Jesus tells us that God knows the number of hairs on our head. Realize there are no details of your life so inconsequential that God finds them not worth remembering. Every mundane detail of your life is given the glory and honor of God's attention.

At this early depth of friendship, we are merely reflecting this characteristic of God toward one another. We are telling someone, "If it happened to you, it's interesting to me because we're friends."

A FEW QUESTIONS TO ASK

As we explore each new depth of friendship, we will end with a few questions. Often, these will be questions you might ask a friend.

Other times, they will be questions to ask yourself and discuss with a friend. Think of these as brainstorming prompts. *Please feel free to add at the end of each chapter more questions that sound like you.*

- Where are you from? What was your journey from there to here?
- What does a normal week look like for you?
- Who are the important people in your life?

Chapter 2

WHAT'S YOUR STORY? THE MAJOR THEMES

DEPTH TWO

Facts congeal into themes as they cluster around a passion or become repetitive. Passions can be either pleasant aspirations we pursue, like our goals, or unpleasant aversions we avoid, like our fears. Repetitions are simply the people and tasks that keep showing up in life. Intuitively, we all realize that some life facts carry more weight than others. As we go deeper in our friendships, we get to know what those weightier facts-turned-themes are.

Our friend probably doesn't use the narrative language of *theme* to describe these aspects of their story. A friend might call them roles, passions, dreams, burdens, aspirations, setbacks, sticky emotions, a sense of calling, or responsibilities. Whatever your friend calls them, any book on making friends and influencing people would tell you that you should ask about these things and listen well when you do. Listening is incarnational—it is how we enter our friend's world.

When we enter someone's home, we take in themes with our eyes. Who's in that picture on the wall? How did you win that award? When did you start that hobby? When we have a conversation, we pick up on themes with our ears. We give our attention.

We resonate with their experience. We "rejoice with those who rejoice, weep with those who weep" (Romans 12:15). We learn about them.

Just as Jesus entered our world when he became an infant, we should strive to enter a friend's world by *compassionately* (as they tell us about hard things) or *co-passionately* (as they share good things) resonating with their experience.

Story themes are excellent opportunities to deepen a friendship. A small gift related to an area of passion, a text that remembers a consistent challenge, prayer for a burden, or questions about a role, all convey, "I see you. I remember the things that are important to you. You matter." This is a primary implication of Ecclesiastes 4:9–12:

> Two are better than one, because they have a good reward for their toil. For if they fall, one will lift up his fellow. But woe to him who is alone when he falls and has not another to lift him up! Again, if two lie together, they keep warm, but how can one keep warm alone? And though a man might prevail against one who is alone, two will withstand him—a threefold cord is not quickly broken.

Good times are richer because of a friend. Hard times are more manageable with a friend. A friend who knows the themes of my life well enough to be aware of both is a treasure.

As we think about the themes in our life story and friendship, we notice something about the relationship between time and friendship. Tenure matters. If you try to pick out themes after two or three conversations, you're acting more like a therapist than a friend. That's a different role.

In friendship, we may ask about themes, but more often we'll notice them as they emerge over time. We don't guess at them ("Do you think you get annoyed by my intrusive questions because of your hyper inquisitive mother?") as if it were our role to *discover* them. Our friend gets to *disclose* them when ready.

But as we get to know the themes of each other's lives, our ability to be friends for one another grows. When we only know the facts of each other's lives, we can only care for each other in surface-level service ways (which is still great). As we get know the themes of each other's stories, we connect and care at deeper relational levels.

A FEW QUESTIONS TO ASK

- What do you know more about than the average person?
- When and how did the things you are passionate about become important to you?
- What goes on the short list of things you never want to neglect?

Chapter 3

WHAT'S YOUR STORY? THE PLOT TWISTS

DEPTH THREE

When did your story zig while you expected it to zag? I remember being an immature high school student with good grades in math, which lead me to initially major in computer science in college. Then Calculus 1 happened. God used a prolonged experience of academic flailing to humble me and graciously redirect me toward a double major in Christian ministry and psychology. Life zigged.

I also remember being a Christian sports camp leader in college. If I do say so myself, I was an excellent baseball coach and Bible study leader. The next summer, the camp asked me to be a camp director. I was ecstatic about the promotion and had lots of great ideas. But then I struggled mightily in the role. I did an adequate job, but my perfectionistic tendencies were not okay with *adequate*. Life zigged again.

From this I decided I was a number two leader, not a number one leader. I was a subleader, not the point guy. After seminary, I came on staff at a parachurch counseling center. After a while, they asked me to be the executive director. I didn't want it. It felt like a setup to fail again. It happened anyway, and I flourished. The ministry grew and I loved it. Life zagged this time.

I'm not unique. All our stories have plot twists. The thing about these moments is not only that they're unexpected, but that they're usually significant. The direction of our life or our sense of identity changes in these moments. Our choices and responses to these moments either significantly enhance or detract from our quality of life.

These are the times when we realize we are not flat, two-dimensional characters. What's a flat character? Think of the old cartoon *Winnie the Pooh*. In those stories, each character is one thing. Owl is the wise sage. Tigger is the impulsive extrovert. Piglet is the faithful worrier. Eeyore is the lovable pessimist. Two-dimensional characters like those never surprise you.

But look at a real life—my life. I surprised myself. First, I wasn't the smart kid I thought I was. Later, I wasn't the leader I thought I would be. Eventually, I found a leadership role I didn't think I could fill but excelled in.

Casual friends become transformative friends—the kind of friend that significantly shapes our lives in godly ways—as they get to know these key junctures in our story. Plot twists reveal our insecurities, points of pride, misconceptions, and responses to surprises. These are qualities friends need to know if we are to "stir up one another to love and good works" (Hebrews 10:24).

A friend who knows about the plot twists in my life can be a help to me when similar situations arise.

- Knowing my math and camp plot twists, a friend might say something like, "I'm not sure you're thinking this decision through well. It seems like you're assuming success in one area means you'll excel in the other. Have you thought about the difference in these two roles/situations?"
- Or with my counseling plot twist in mind, the friend might encourage me with, "It seems like you may be discounting

the ways you've matured since the last time an opportunity like this came along. You don't have to assume that because the first opportunity didn't go as well as you wanted any leadership role is too much for you."

As friends, we won't always guess right in our encouragements or cautions. But knowing the plot twists in each other's lives gives us a more complete context for speaking into each other's lives.

Have you and your friends shared these junctures of your lives with each other? It makes for some great conversations. You should consider it.

A FEW QUESTIONS TO ASK

- When did life zig while you expected it to zag?
- What were the moments in your life when, for better or worse, you surprised yourself most?
- What are the things you enjoy that least fit your personality or strongest aptitudes?

Chapter 4

WHAT'S YOUR STORY? THE LIFE-SHAPING EVENTS

DEPTH FOUR

We've been trying to go incrementally deeper in our friendships. But for some of us, asking and sharing about life-shaping events may feel like a leap. Not all life-shaping, depth-four experiences are created equal. Some weigh a hundred pounds of joy. Others are fifty pounds of satisfaction and fifty pounds of sadness. Still others feel like five hundred pounds of angst.

Some painful life-shaping events might actually be depth five (or beyond). Remember, the roots metaphor with its various depths is there to serve us, to illustrate our journey. We shouldn't become slaves to the metaphor.

The things we'll begin to discuss at this depth of friendship are the BC versus AD moments of our lives—the events that have a *before* and *after* effect on how we tell our story. These are the moments that profoundly shaped our lives.

Some of these are happy events (conversion, getting married, getting your dream job). Some are painful and may be disruptive to talk about even now (a divorce, an experience of abuse). Others can be strongly mixed (empty nest, retirement from a job you loved).

Because of this variance, deciding *what* to disclose *when* is not just about the depth of your friendship; it is also about your readiness to share. Don't feel rushed. Getting to this point in a book is not the same thing as being at that point in your personal journey.

This is another reason not every friendship needs to be at depth thirty-five. We don't have all thirty-five friendships because we are finite people who live within the confines of a 168-hour week. We also don't have all thirty-five friendships because it would be overwhelming to share that much of our story with all our friends.

This book's root framework gives you two things to help you determine when to take a friendship to this depth:

1. **A gauge** to tell if you have laid the appropriate foundation.
2. **A plan** for deepening friendships in other areas to prepare the way for confiding these experiences.

You might ask, "How might sharing these heavy things with a friend benefit me?" That's not a selfish question. It's just cautious. The answer is (at least in part) that it removes a sense of secrecy, stigma, and shame. When we're ready, there is relief in knowing we don't have to hide part of our story from the people most meaningfully involved in our lives. We'll explore these themes more in question 3, "What's hard?"

But not all depth-four experiences in your stories are heavy. Many are happy. Sharing these parts of our stories have immense value as well. When you know the pleasant pivot points in my life, you can share in my joys and celebrate God's goodness in those moments with me. We share the good times of our lives because they are evidence of God's grace, provision, and care.

Take a moment. Think through the high-highs and low-lows we read throughout the Bible. For the CliffsNotes version, read Hebrews 11. These aren't fictional stories like *Aesop's Fables*. These are real, lived experiences of people like us. Their stories made it into the Bible, at least in part because they had the courage to share them. What felt scary and intimidating to them is an example and source of encouragement to us.

This brings us to an atypical question about the Bible: are we as honest as our Bible? Often in church, we are used to being asked if we read our Bible. This is a different question. As you read your Bible, ask yourself, "Am I as honest with my friends about my life as these people were about theirs?" The Bible both gives *instruction* to learn from and *examples* to follow that show what it looks like to participate in the family of God.

A FEW QUESTIONS TO ASK

- What are the BC versus AD moments in your life?
- What primary life lessons have you taken from these events?
- What ways have you learned to trust and rely on God in light of these pivotal moments?

Chapter 5

WHAT'S YOUR STORY? THE POINT OF YOUR STORY

DEPTH FIVE

There is something that happens as a friendship progresses from depth one to depth five. *Our friend becomes less and less an observer of our story and more and more a participant in our story.* The deepening roots of story help us understand why this happens.

Our stories are living stories that are still being written. But because they are living stories, they don't just have characters, settings, plots, and plot twists. They have direction, trajectory, and purpose. They have a point. For Christians, our lives were meant for more than pursuing our curiosities. Our lives are meant to be salt and light: "Let your light shine before others, so that they may see your good works and give glory to your Father who is in heaven" (Matthew 5:16).

Being salt and light are very context-specific functions. For the church to be the light of the world, we must shine where we live. If the church is going to be the salt of the earth, we must flavor Christlikeness in our specific spheres of influence. As each Christian fulfills their individual salt-and-light function where they live, they contribute to Christ's commission for the church at large in the world at large.

Good Christian friends ask each other about these godly purposes and goals—the point of their stories:

1. **Salt Function:** Where, how, and with whom am I spreading a Christlike flavor?
2. **Light Function:** Where, how, and with whom am I serving as a beacon for the light of God's truth?

The answer can be as simple as faithfully attending a small group, discipling my family, and witnessing to my coworkers. Or the answer can be as bold as becoming a church planter among an unreached people group. However ordinary or bold, the answers should be clearly known by your close friends.

There are two implications for what we have covered so far:

1. You should know the point of your friend's story and vice versa.
2. The deeper your friendship, the more you participate in and influence each other's stories.

As friendship deepens, we don't listen to each other's stories like we read a good novel. When we read a novel, the story is complete, fully edited, unalterable. The only suspense that exists is because we have yet to turn the last page.

Good friends listen to each other's stories like guest editors in the draft phase of writing a novel. We don't get a metaphorical pen—it's their life. They make the choices for their story, and good friends honor each other's autonomy. But we do ask questions, offer feedback, and encourage the process. We *want* our friend's story to reach its desired conclusion because we're vested characters in it.

To fill this role effectively, we need to know the point of our friend's story. What do they want to do with their life? How would our friend complete the sentence, "When this chapter of my life concludes, I will be disappointed if ________"?

We tie our guest editor contributions to this purpose. Otherwise, we're just offering our superfluous opinions about what we would do if their story were our story. There's nothing wrong with that, but anybody at a coffee shop can do that.

As we live inside our friend's story, our transformative task is to ask, "Is this chapter of your story staying true to what you intended it to do? Are you stewarding your gifts, relationships, and opportunities toward the passions God gave you?" When we promote someone from a casual acquaintance to transformative friend, we are giving them permission to be a guest editor who helps us keep our bearings, so our story doesn't drift into something inconsequential.

A FEW QUESTIONS TO ASK

- How do you complete the sentence, "When this season of my life concludes, I will be disappointed if ________"?
- Whose lives do you want to be different because of this season of your life?
- How can I encourage and help you in these things?

Summative Exercise 1

A MIDDLE-SCHOOL-LEVEL BOOK REVIEW

Do you remember doing book reviews when you were twelve? Your teacher gave you a few questions that became an outline for a paper to determine how well you understood a piece of literature. These questions were things like:

- Who is the **main character**? What is he/she like?
- Where does the story take place? What's significant about the **setting**?
- What is the **goal** the main character is trying to achieve or the **problem** he/she is trying to overcome?
- Who are the **supporting characters**? Which supporting character is aiding the main character toward their goal, and which ones are hindering, and how?
- What is the **point of the story**? What message makes sense of the events?

These questions don't just help us dissect books; they help us get to know people. Ask yourself, can I do a middle-school-level book review of my friend's life? Can my friend do one for my life?

We begin to realize how surface-level our knowledge of each other is. We know recent events and a few standout qualities, but we don't tie them in with our friend's larger story. Because of this we remain benevolent observers of each other's lives. We don't become friends embedded in each other's stories.

Saying it that way, we realize God wants more from our relationships in the church. Consider how Paul described his relationships within the church in 1 Thessalonians 2:8. "So, being affectionately desirous of you, we were ready to share with you not only the gospel of God *but also our own selves, because you had become very dear to us*" (emphasis added).

We won't get there with surface-level conversations. But we can get there by intentionally going deeper in our existing friendships. Imagine if the people in your small group knew each other at a middle-school-book-review level? Don't gloss over the implications of that question.

How would knowing each other that way deepen your experience of church? How would it affect your level of engagement in prayer times? How would it impact the kinds of things you text each other? How would it multiply the number of things you celebrate together? How would it expand the amount of support and understanding you have in hard times? How would it make church feel more like family?

As we imagine this, we're not imagining Narnia, a fantasy land of fauns, dryads, and unicorns. We're envisioning what God intends the church to be. Here are three ways you can bridge the gap between our current experience and God's design for Christian friendships in the area of story.

- Set aside time in small group once a month and invite someone to share their story, not just their conversion testimony (although that should be a significant part of it), but their life story. Intentionally set aside the time to know each other this way because you value it.
- Invite a Christian friend at work, school, the gym, or a comparable setting to read this book with you. Transformative friendships don't happen by accident. Extend an invitation.

- If you have an accountability partner, consider broadening your relationship to include the full scope of things we're discussing in this book. Chances are the relationship will endure longer and have a greater impact if you do.

Question Two: What's Good?

Depth One: Your Talents

Depth Two: Your Quirks

Depth Three: Your Roles

Depth Four: Your Sacrifices

Depth Five: Your Character

As Christians, we sometimes get so excited about the power of the gospel to forgive sin that we become preoccupied with the bad in each other's lives. While our intentions are good, being preoccupied with what is bad can make Christian friendship feel heavy.

Questions two, three, and four in our seven simple questions will explore the *good*, the *hard*, and the *bad* in each other's lives. We're not avoiding the bad. But we are starting where the Bible starts: "And God saw everything that he had made, and behold, it was very good" (Genesis 1:31). The bad is bad because it distorts and disrupts the good. The more we see the good in each other, the more motivated we will be to forsake the bad.

The simple question, "What's good?" affirms three truths about our Christian friend:

1. God made you in intricate detail: "I am fearfully and wonderfully made" (Psalm 139:14).
2. God gave you unique talents: "There are varieties of gifts, but the same Spirit; and there are varieties of service, but the

same Lord; and there are varieties of activities, but it is the same God who empowers them all in everyone" (1 Corinthians 12:4–6).

3. God's design *of* you coincides with God's purpose *for* you: "We are his workmanship, created in Christ Jesus for good works, which God prepared beforehand, that we should walk in them" (Ephesians 2:10).

Believing these things about our friend produces a pleasant curiosity. Curiosity says, "You're worth knowing," and friendship grows as we learn.

It's worth noting that the curiosity of a friend is different from the questions of a counselor. Counselors ask systematic questions to glean a thorough history and assess the origins of a problem. One person asks, the other answers. There is a helper and one who is helped. But friends ask curious questions along the way as life happens. Both friends ask, both friends answer. To the degree that roles exist, there are two helpers and two recipients of help.

I make this caveat because I am a counselor writing about friendship. But I'm not trying to change your friendships into therapeutic relationships. Both are good and have their place. I like being a counselor. But in these pages, we're cultivating friendships.

In this section, we're asking, "What's good?" to spur growth *toward virtue* more than *away from vice*. In churches, we often say, "You replicate what you celebrate." The principle is that when you verbally draw attention to a good action, people are more likely to repeat that good action.

To get a sense of the power of this, imagine a social context where it was the habit of everyone to catch others doing good things. Further, imagine it was their habit to verbally affirm the person caught doing a good thing. What would it be like to live in that world?

Most of us answer, "I don't know. That sounds too good to be true." What we dismiss as utopia is the reality God intends for the church to be. Describing the early church, Paul wrote, "Therefore encourage one another and build one another up, just as you are doing" (1 Thessalonians 5:11). Paul caught them catching one another being Christlike and affirming each other for it. He affirmed them for affirming one another. It was a beautifully virtuous cycle.

Our exploration of *what's good* is intended to transform the culture of our friendships to match the culture Paul saw in the Thessalonians. Yearn for it, and let's explore how to make it happen.

Chapter 6

WHAT'S GOOD? YOUR TALENTS

DEPTH ONE

From an early age, most of us notice *who* is good at *what*. We identify the smart kids, the funny kids, the fast kids, the strong kids, the nice kids, the rule-abiding kids, etc. Depth one under *what's good* is so obvious we almost can't prevent ourselves from noticing it. So, our goal here is simply to take these observations from unspoken to spoken.

We want it to become our habit to frequently say things like, "You did a great job of ________," or "I've noticed you're exceptional at ________," or "I appreciate the time and attention you give to ________."

For some of us, the obstacle to deepening friendship is figuring out how to respond to affirmations like these without being awkward. Saying thank you isn't the equivalent of arrogantly saying, "I know," but to some of us it feels that way.

Don't overthink it. Relax, smile, and just say thank you. Otherwise, compliments become hard breaks that change the cadence of a conversation. Warmly receive the affirmation and allow the conversation to continue in the direction it was going.

Another depth-one obstacle under *what's good* is that, even as adults, we all live with bit of the residue of adolescence in our souls. In our teenage years, social pressure made it feel like we were competing in the Standout Attribute Olympics. "I like this *about* you," often meant "I like you *because of* this." Now that we are more mature, we want to affirm people in a way that says, "I enjoy your quick wit," not, "I am your friend because you're funny."

The easiest and most edifying way to do this is to notice your friend's whole character, not just their standout qualities. When we realize the power of simple affirmations, we see the importance of looking for and affirming the whole character of Christ in our friends.

Take lists of the good in the Bible and turn them into a scavenger hunt in your friends.

- The list of the fruit of Spirit in Galatians 5:22–23: love, joy, peace, patience, kindness, goodness, faithfulness, gentleness, and self-control.
- The list of love's qualities in 1 Corinthians 13:4–7: it is patient, kind, not envious, not boastful, not arrogant, not rude, not insistent on its own way, not rejoicing in wrongdoing but in truth, sustaining, believing, hoping, and enduring.
- The list of praiseworthy things to think about in Philippians 4:8–9: whatever is true, honorable, just, pure, lovely, commendable, and excellent.
- The list of nonintuitive virtues that are the Beatitudes in Matthew 5:3–12: poverty of spirit, mourning, meekness, a hunger and thirst for righteousness, mercy, purity of heart, peacemaking, and persecution for righteousness.

Play "good gotcha" as you spend time with your friends. Doing this helps us break the tendency toward strength-cliquing, where we socialize primarily with those who share our strengths. If we want friendships to transform our lives (and that's why we're reading this book), then we must have friends who are strong where we're weak and who value what we tend to neglect.

Getting away from strength-cliquing changes us in two important ways. The first may be more obvious. But the second is more powerful.

1. **Observation:** As we *see* friends do well at what we're weaker at, we *learn* from them. Emulating people we admire is a common way to grow.
2. **Acclimation:** Having friends who are strong where we are weak also gives us a context to *grow more comfortable with our weaknesses being known*. This is liberating. No more impostor syndrome! No more image management!

Surprisingly, for many of us, the key word for depth one under *what's good* may be *courage*. Have the courage to notice your friends' strengths rather than feeling insecure in comparison to them. Friendship is not a competition. Friendship is being on each other's team. Embrace this and allow it to give you the freedom to cheer your friends on where they excel.

A FEW QUESTIONS TO ASK

- What are you good at or enjoy that many people don't see?
- What are things that people think you work harder at than you actually do?
- What is the best (most receivable) way for me to encourage you?

Chapter 7
WHAT'S GOOD? YOUR QUIRKS
DEPTH TWO

Sometimes the good things in our lives are also things that make us blush. My wife, Sallie, is one of the most organized people I have ever met. I regularly tell her, "Thank you for all the things I never have to think about." So much in our home just gets done because of her immaculate systems.

For example, our home is littered, in the best sense of that word, with love notes. These notes don't have hearts and sweet talk on them. They have tasks, reminders, and due dates to indicate what needs to be done and when. Sallie describes these things as her compulsions (in the nonclinical use of this term) and apologizes saying, "I'm sorry you live in a house with so many notes."

These are Sallie-quirks. To me and our boys, they are highly endearing. We don't know how our home would function without them. For Sallie, it is something she can easily become self-conscious about. These are the kinds of things we affirm at depth two under *what's good*. They are the quirks that those who love us find endearing but that we might feel self-conscious about.

Use your imagination again. What would it be like to live in a world where you didn't feel compelled to hide your quirks? That's the world we're creating.

You might ask, does the Bible give evidence of these kinds of interactions? The answer is yes if we know where and how to look. If we only read our Bible *seriously*, we only find serious things. But if we read our Bible *playfully*, we observe some of these lighthearted interactions.

Have you ever noticed that many of the disciples had nicknames? There were the Sons of Thunder (Mark 3:17). They were the bit-too-passionate disciples whose emotions tended to run away with them. There was "Thomas, called the Twin" (John 11:16). Many early traditions say this was not because Thomas had a biological twin but because Thomas was a doppelganger for Jesus. There was John, "the disciple whom Jesus loved" (John 21:20). Teacher's pet! You get the sense that the disciples really enjoyed one another and had fun with their quirks. They could laugh *with*, not *at*, one another.

Depth two under *what's good* is, in large part, about edifying humor—the ability to acknowledge our idiosyncrasies in a way that is uplifting. This is important because none of us is normal. In reality, *normal* is a word like *unicorn*. We know what it means, and we know it doesn't exist. Healthy friendship is a place where we're okay with that.

In depth two we're creating an atmosphere of grace: friendships where we're increasingly known, quirks and all, and accepted. This entails crossing the emotional barrier of vulnerability about things like being a little too list and organization dependent. Yes, there will be bigger barriers to cross. But if you haven't crossed this one yet, you can consider it next to do.

A FEW QUESTIONS TO ASK

- What's something you tend to be embarrassed about that you don't need to be?

- Who are the people that respond best to your quirks? Who responds poorly?
- How can I make sure I don't aggravate your insecurity about these things in our friendship?

Chapter 8

WHAT'S GOOD? YOUR ROLES

DEPTH THREE

Roles don't tend to be exciting. To become a role, something must be daily, regular, or common. As such, these activities and functions often get taken for granted. When something becomes a role, it usually only gets noticed when we mess up. Roles easily become discouragement-only parts of life. We want to change that at depth three under *what's good*.

Write a list of your primary roles: student, employee, boss, son, daughter, sibling, spouse, parent, teacher, friend, etc. Chances are, at least 80 percent of God's will for your life is simply fulfilling these roles with excellence. Too often, when we think of God's will for our life, we think of the atypical opportunities. We look for God's will in the exceptional rather than the ordinary, in the arhythmic rather than the rhythmic parts of life.

Intentional friendship is a great place to change that. In a good friendship, we encourage and affirm faithfulness in fulfilling the mundane parts of life. In a deepening friendship, we should notice the parts of each other's lives that more casual acquaintances overlook. This is a large part of what makes these deepening friendships both more ordinary *and* more important.

Notice the affirmation that God gives Bezalel in Exodus 31:2–5: "See, I have called by name Bezalel the son of Uri, son of Hur, of the tribe of Judah, and I have filled him with the Spirit of God, with ability and intelligence, with knowledge and all craftsmanship, to devise artistic designs, to work in gold, silver, and bronze, in cutting stones for setting, and in carving wood, to work in every craft."

This introduction starts excitingly. When God calls you by name and recites your family lineage, you're expecting a Moses-esque assignment. But then the description gets progressively less interesting. By the end, Bezalel gets the woodcarving Boy Scout badge. Most of his workday would have been spent in the shop working with metal, stones, and wood.

But this doesn't diminish the affirmation he received from God or the admiration of his friends. To Bezalel, filling his role was daily. To God and his friends, his work was exceptional. We live in the same tension with our roles. *Filled faithfully*, each role makes a profound difference, but *lived daily*, we get bored and feel inconsequential.

Friends are God's agents to respeak life into stale roles. It may be as simple as a "How's it going with ______?" question that shows this part of your friend's life isn't forgotten. It may be a word of commendation about faithfulness in that role. It may be listening to a story about that role with fresh attention. While simple, these actions breathe freshness into stale parts of life.

A FEW QUESTIONS TO ASK

- What important parts of your week do you tend to get most bored or discouraged with?
- When in your week would it be most meaningful for me to encourage you in these roles?
- What was it that originally made you excited about embracing each role?

Chapter 9

WHAT'S GOOD? YOUR SACRIFICES

DEPTH FOUR

Roles aren't free. Saying yes to one thing requires saying no to a dozen other things. If we are going to faithfully fill the roles God has called us to, we are going to make sacrifices. The dailiness of roles results in these sacrifices often going unnoticed. Although unnoticed, our faithfulness in these sacrifices is good and merits affirmation.

Who knows the rhythms of your life roles? Who asks about the accompanying sacrifices—not just about the burden of them, but the things that make the sacrifice worth it to you? Whose sacrifices do you know and ask about?

Too often, the answer is no one. That's why we're bringing intentionality to our friendships. Most of us have regular areas of sacrifice that no one ever asks about. This isn't a problem to be fixed as much as a facet of our life to be known. We are weary not because these sacrifices are too heavy or unfair, but because we're carrying them alone.

Growing a deeper friendship in this way has a wonderful bitterness-prevention effect. Here, we're not talking about bitterness that erupts from major offense, but the bitterness that accumulates after prolonged exhaustion. Feeling known is an excellent balm against feeling used. The compassionate and curious ear of a good friend can do wonders to build our resilience.

In Luke 9:23, Jesus calls us to die to ourselves daily. Many of us do this in variety of ways just by living out our daily rhythms. But when we feel unseen, these daily sacrifices can accumulate into a big ball of discontentment and martyrdom. While these daily sacrifices may not be that heavy, when unnoticed, we can feel like we're suffocating under a proverbial ton of feathers.

When this happens, we vacillate between (1) dismissing our reaction as overly dramatic and (2) feeling desperate. Even if our unknown sacrifices are small and we were glad to make them (at least at first), unnoticed, they feel unsustainable. One moment we chastise ourselves for being a wimp and selfish, the next we elevate our hardship to the status of martyr and view those who benefit from our sacrifice as oppressors. In both moments, guilt and anger, we are fully convinced we're right.

What's the way out? We need to get these ping-ponging emotions out of our own head and into a conversation with a friend. Yes, we may need to make some helpful, logistical changes: redistributing tasks, talking with someone who is taking us for granted, or remembering why we first agreed to these sacrifices. But the value of being heard often does more for our morale than these logistical changes.

Two things can be true at the same time: your sacrifices are *heavy*, and your sacrifices are *good*. You don't have to choose. But a choice worth making is to elevate a depth-three friend to depth four by saying something like this: "You know me. You know the people, roles, and causes that are important to me. Recently, life has gotten heavy and I'm not sure if I'm overcommitted, have a bad attitude, or if this is just a difficult season. But I value our friendship and I would appreciate you helping me think it through. Can we talk about it?"

A statement like this takes you from alone to supported. When you're struggling to endure under the good sacrifices of roles you gladly embraced, instead of just white-knuckling through, phone a friend.

A FEW QUESTIONS TO ASK

- What sacrifices that you willingly make go unnoticed most often?
- What makes these sacrifices worth it to you?
- When do these sacrifices tend to weigh on you most?

Chapter 10

WHAT'S GOOD? YOUR CHARACTER

DEPTH FIVE

In sports, it is understood that there's a difference between having a great day and being a great player. We all have that friend who frequently reflects, "Do you remember *that game* I had my junior year of high school? It was awesome. If a college scout had been there, I know I would have gotten a scholarship offer. Might have gone pro."

But it's not just athletics. This same distinction exists between doing a good deed and having a godly character. Helping an old lady across the street in third grade doesn't mean your hometown should rename the community center after you.

A tenured, vested friend—the kind of friend being cultivated in this book—is in a unique position to offer perspective on your character. As you journey through these seven questions together, the friend gets to know how you respond to good times, hard times, setbacks, promotions, and stagnation. The friend sees you with family, friends, strangers, and adversaries. The friend calls you on your sin, encourages you in your suffering, and reminds you of your identity in Christ.

Friendships like that, forged over time, offer a perspective that is more valuable than diamonds. Their commentary on your character isn't rooted in what you did or didn't do in a moment, but in what they've observed over years, in a variety of settings, with a variety of people. They know who you are, what it took to get there, and how far you've come. They are also excited about where God is taking you.

This is the kind of relationship Paul and Timothy shared. It is what compelled Paul to write, "I thank God whom I serve, as did my ancestors, with a clear conscience, as I remember you constantly in my prayers night and day. As I remember your tears, I long to see you, that I may be filled with joy. I am reminded of your sincere faith, a faith that dwelt first in your grandmother Lois and your mother Eunice and now, I am sure, dwells in you as well" (2 Timothy 1:3–5).

As Christians, we should talk this way to one another. These kinds of comments shouldn't be reserved for wedding toasts and retirement roasts. Conversations like this should echo between friends, between spouses, and between parents and children throughout the church. We should affirm those we know well, specifically and personally.

In his words to Timothy, Paul does three things that give us an example to follow.

1. Paul expresses joy and thankfulness about their friendship.
2. Paul is specific about what he is affirming—in this case, the sincerity of Timothy's faith.
3. Paul traces the lineage of what he is affirming. He compares it to the faith of two influential women in Timothy's life, his mother and grandmother.

If you have a friendship ready to graduate to depth five under *what's good*, do what Paul did. Take time to think about your friendship. Identify the godly character qualities in your friend. Name them. Cite the history of how you've seen those character qualities develop. Celebrate what God is doing in and through your friend that you are in a unique position to see and affirm. If you want to go deeper in a meaningful friendship, get out a piece of paper and start drafting something now.

A FEW QUESTIONS TO ASK

Note: These questions are more prompts for a meaningful letter than for an impromptu conversation. As friendships deepen, not all meaningful interactions will be spontaneous or verbal.

- What qualities of Christlikeness do you see most clearly or uniquely in your friend?
- How have you seen these qualities develop over time?
- How have you been blessed by these qualities in your friend?

Summative Exercise 2

SPONTANEOUS, SPECIFIC AFFIRMATIONS

With some summative exercises we will go deep, targeting depth-five engagement. But for this summative exercise, we are going to go broad. You are being invited to live life on a scavenger hunt, and the character of Christ is the scorecard.

Perhaps you've been at an event where a scavenger hunt was used as an icebreaker. The scorecard asked you to find someone with a birthday in the same month as yours, or find someone born west of the Mississippi River, and so on. You win the game by being the first person to find someone with each characteristic.

A scavenger hunt requires you to be verbal and interactive, to initiate conversations. So does this summative exercise. Here is the scorecard:

- Identify when a friend shows a Christlike quality.
- Identify when a friend rests well in God's care during a difficult time.
- Identify when a friend uses a God-given talent to bless someone else.
- Identify when a friend embodies a New Testament one-another command.
- Identify when a friend lives out the wisdom of Proverbs.
- You get the idea. Find a friend who is bringing the Bible to life.

But in this game, it's not enough to write the friend's name on a piece of paper beside each item. Tell your friend. Be specific about what you noticed. Spark a church culture where no Christlike quality goes unaffirmed. The principle is to *replicate* Christlikeness throughout your peer group, *celebrate* Christlikeness wherever you see it.

Beyond this perpetual game of "good gotcha," consider adding a less impromptu version. In your small group or on your ministry team, start to keep track of when people first join. Each year on their anniversary, invite fellow group members to affirm the godly qualities they've seen in the person over the past year.

These affirmations may be shared verbally or collected in writing. Either way, create a culture of being *vigilant for godliness* and *expressive with encouragement*. For those who did not grow up in homes where these kinds of interactions were normal, getting to hear this done on a regular basis helps them experience the kind of family God wanted them to have. Their church is becoming their family as you do this. Friends are becoming brothers and sisters in Christ. Biblical metaphors are becoming reality.

Question Three: What's Hard?

Depth One: The Flip Side of Your Strengths

Depth Two: Your Current Life Challenges

Depth Three: The Fall Around You

Depth Four: The Fall Within You

Depth Five: What You've Never Told Anyone

What's hard is about unlearning the understandable but misguided fallacy that if something is not good it must be bad. Can *hard* and *bad* be the same thing? Sure. But we miss something very significant if we always treat them as synonyms.

Bad means morally wrong. Hard means emotionally, relationally, or logistically difficult. Christians often default to interpreting hard as bad because it would be clearer to identify how Jesus is the answer if hard were bad. But the result is that we feel guilty for things that are not wrong, and we ask God to forgive us when he actually wants to comfort us.

Proverbs 17:17 tells us, "A friend loves at all times" (that means good, bad, and hard times), "and a brother is born for adversity" (hard times). What does this mean? It means there is a unique and irreplaceable benefit from friendship when life is hard. Our goal, in this section, is to give you the tools to begin mining these benefits in your friendships.

By separating question three, "What's hard?" from question four, "What's bad?" we're distinguishing sin from suffering. We are both sinners and sufferers. Both sin and suffering have their origin in the Genesis 3 account of the fall, when Adam and Eve first disobeyed God, resulting in evil, shame, curses, death, and all the other unpleasant experiences of our lives. Both sin and suffering represent a distortion of God's original and good creation. When we pray, "Your kingdom come, your will be done, on earth as it is in heaven" (Matthew 6:10), we are praying against both sin and suffering.

So, what's the difference between them? When we get to question four, "What's bad?" we'll be looking at those life disruptions that emerge from our unbiblical beliefs, values, and choices. There is hope for these things. That hope is called repentance. We should be grateful for this hope and talk about it openly with our friends.

But in this section, we will be considering the hardships that emerge from living in a fallen world, among fallen people, in fallen bodies. There is hope for these things too. There is *ultimate hope* when Jesus finally wipes away every tear, "and death shall be no more, neither shall there be mourning, nor crying, nor pain anymore, for the former things have passed away" (Revelation 21:4). And there is *temporal hope* as we share the load with one another and seek to find meaning amid our hardships. But even when we're faithful, life is still hard sometimes.

There is one more clarification you may need to hear. When you acknowledge suffering, you are not succumbing to passivity. Sometimes Christians avoid classifying a struggle as suffering because we fear this means there's nothing we can do about it. Just because there is nothing we *could have done* to prevent suffering doesn't mean there is nothing we *can do* now to alleviate its effects.

We are right to recognize that the pivotal difference between sin and suffering is personal agency. I am responsible for my sin. I do my sin. I am not responsible for my suffering. Suffering happens to me. But so does the weather. And when it rains (if my wife warns me), I pack an umbrella. When it's cold, I wear a coat. The weather happens to me, and I can't change it, but I'm not passive toward it.

One of the most proactive things we can do with our suffering is talk about it with a trusted friend. A litany of options emerges for how to respond wisely from there. Once we have the support of a friend, we don't have to brainstorm or enact those options on our own. That makes a world of difference.

Chapter 11
WHAT'S HARD?
THE FLIP SIDE OF YOUR STRENGTHS
DEPTH ONE

It is said that most weaknesses are exaggerated strengths. Are you highly organized? Chances are you're prone to be slightly controlling. Are you great with people? You likely struggle to stay on schedule. Are you a natural leader? You are probably overbearing at times. Are you highly compassionate? Chances are you struggle with people-pleasing. Any strength has an inherent weakness.

The least invasive way to talk about what's hard is usually to talk about these weaknesses that correspond with our strengths. Can the examples we listed above become sin? Yes. But the tendencies behind those sins are often just hard. Responded to well, these weakness-temptations are opportunities for God's strength to be "made perfect in weakness" (2 Corinthians 12:9). The sooner we talk about these challenges, the less likely we are to need to repent of their sinful mutations.

Think back to depth one under *what's good*, where you explored strengths. Think about your own strengths, and then ask yourself, *If I'm good at those things, what are the corresponding weaknesses?* Now ask, *Who knows about these weaknesses, not because they're affected by them, but because I initiated a conversation?*

Most of us respond, *Well, yuck! This isn't fun.* You might protest, *I thought this was a book on friendship.*

Can you catch the logical fallacy in these two responses? It assumes that everything about friendship is fun, pleasant, and enjoyable. It is true that friendship is good, edifying, and transformative. But sometimes good feels awkward. That's okay. You'll get good at awkward as we take this journey together. Actually, healthy awkward is excellent at preventing bad.

Let's take our friend, Simon "The Rock" Peter. What was Peter's strength? Boldness. What was Peter's corresponding weakness? Putting his foot in his mouth.

- When Jesus explained how he had to go to Jerusalem to suffer and die, "Peter took him aside and began to rebuke him, saying, 'Far be it from you, Lord! This shall never happen to you.' But he turned and said to Peter, 'Get behind me, Satan! You are a hindrance to me'" (Matthew 16:22–23).
- When Peter saw Jesus transfigured and talking with Moses and Elijah, "Peter said to Jesus, 'Rabbi, it is good that we are here. Let us make three tents, one for you and one for Moses and one for Elijah.' For he did not know what to say, for they were terrified. And a cloud overshadowed them, and a voice came out of the cloud, 'This is my beloved Son, listen to him'" (Mark 9:5–7).

When God from heaven has to say (to paraphrase), "Shhh! Now is the time for listening, not talking," you know you've drifted to the weakness side of boldness.

You know what's awesome about this? It made it into the Bible. As an apostle, Peter read, smiled, shrugged, blushed, and said, "Yeah, that's me—again." The other disciples nodded and started sharing their favorite Peter-didn't-mentally-filter stories.

This is speculation, but it's not far-fetched. These good-natured interactions with his friends about weaknesses fostered the humility and trust that allowed Peter to respond favorably when Paul had to confront him about significant sin in his life (Peter was excluding gentile believers, described in Galatians 2:11–14). Talking about our weaknesses is how we acclimate to acknowledging parts of our life that negatively impact others.

Take the challenge. Ask a friend, "What are my weaknesses and how do they impact you? When am I blind to them and how do I explain them away?" The reality is that your weaknesses exist, and they impact those around you. It's just a matter of whether you talk about them constructively or ignore them until they create a problem and you're more prone to be defensive.

A FEW QUESTIONS TO ASK

- When do you get on your own nerves? What's annoying to you about you?
- When you're trying to do a good thing, what are the common side effects?
- What personal weakness are you most and least comfortable talking about?

Chapter 12

WHAT'S HARD? YOUR CURRENT LIFE CHALLENGES

DEPTH TWO

What's hard gets heavy faster than previous questions. There's no way around it. This is one reason why not every friendship will grow as deep at the same pace. It's common to be at depth four of *what's good* and *what's fun* but still emerging into depth two of *what's hard* and *what's bad*. That's okay. Our journey is about self-awareness and intentionality, not symmetry.

This level of friendship has degrees within depth two. There are mild life challenges and severe life challenges. The challenge if your child neglects schoolwork is less heavy than the challenge of trying to convince your child to go to rehab. But while one is heavier, neither is light.

To appreciate this, we must remember that *suffering is not a competitive sport*. Just because someone else is battling cancer doesn't mean your chronic migraines are less painful. We're not competing for compassion from God or our friends. (If you struggle to have constructive conversations about suffering because of misunderstandings like this, consider the article "Making Peace with Romans 8:28" at bradhambrick.com/romans828.)

When we get caught in the whose-suffering-is-worse mindset, we often hold back from sharing because we think we're whining. It may be helpful to think this way: prayer is constructively taking our worries to God. Whining is potential prayer. It has much of the same content as prayer but lacks a Godward direction. In that sense, whining is worrying that has become ingrown like a toenail, instead of being taken to God.

Confiding in a friend is between these two options, but on the positive side of the midpoint. A friend can't answer like God can—not with God's perfect compassion and power. But often, a conversation with a good friend is like a prayer rehearsal, though not a prayer replacement. We figure out what we want to say.

A theme verse for this depth of friendship is Galatians 6:2, "Bear one another's burdens, and so fulfill the law of Christ." Friends can only share the load with us if we trust them enough to tell them what our load is. Our disclosure is the prerequisite to their ability to fulfill Galatians 6:2.

This verse always reminds me of my favorite passage from *The Lord of the Rings*. The ring bearer Frodo has the duty of carrying the ring of power to Mordor to destroy it, but his friend Samwise is with him. Frodo is exhausted. Sam looks at him and says, "I can't carry it for you, but I can carry you."[1] This beautifully captures the heart and capacity of a friend in hard times.

We can't carry our friend's burden. We can't take it off them. But we can support them. This captures the difference between trying to do life *for* someone and doing life *with* someone. *For* is a mutation of good intentions that robs our friend of their autonomy. It's controlling or codependent. *With* is healthy and encapsulates biblical friendship.

What does it take to invite a Samwise into your life? It takes the courage to be honest, a willingness to admit you're struggling,

1. J. R. R. Tolkien, *The Return of the King: Being the Third Part of the Lord of the Rings* (London: HarperCollins, 2017, first published 1955), 1230.

and the patience to accept that, even if your friend can't make "it" better, "it" will be lighter when you're not carrying it alone.

Start with the simple request, "Something has been weighing on me. Can we talk about it?" This honors your friend by signaling that they need to be in a posture to hear something heavy. It gets you started talking without there having to be a perfect, natural segue. From there, just talk about it.

A FEW QUESTIONS TO ASK

- How can I pray for you?
- What's been discouraging for you recently?
- What kind of things are persistently hard in your life?

Chapter 13

WHAT'S HARD? THE FALL AROUND YOU

DEPTH THREE

Biblically, whether something is hard or bad, its roots begin with the fall in Genesis 3. That's literally when "all hell broke loose" in this world. Whether it's the evil within us or the hardship around us, Adam's and Eve's shuddering shoulders as they awakened to the impact of eating the forbidden fruit tipped the first domino that has spread heartache through human history.

I remember January of 2018. I was living in North Carolina. But near my hometown at Marshall County High School there was a shooting.[1] I had walked those halls. I had friends whose father pastored in that community. January 2018 echoed the December 1997 shooting at Heath High School, one of the first of these early phenomena of school shootings. I had been all over the Heath High School campus as a graduating senior in 1995. I had travel baseball teammates from that school. Both times, it was surreal to see places on the news that had been so familiar to me.

1. If you are a parent or pastor seeking guidance for caring for students in the aftermath of school violence, consider the series of resources at bradhambrick.com/schoolviolence.

Then there was the massive tornado that hit Mayfield, Kentucky, in 2021, ripping a 260-mile path of destruction. To get home for Christmas that year, my family had to drive through the destruction. I knew those winding country roads well. I knew what they had looked like before. Mile after mile, we saw the remnants of people's lives. How do you process an experience like that?

These are examples of the fall around us. I hadn't been bad. I kind of wished there was something I could repent of that would have made a difference because I would have felt less powerless. But even though I was innocent, I couldn't have a normal day. Focusing on a college lecture, caring for a counseling case, or remembering "the reason for the season" after the tornado were near impossible—even though focus, caring, and remembering are traits I would list as personal strengths.

Each of these events was a national news story. But the fall around us can be much more mundane: getting sick for the third time in two months, a long dark winter that prompts seasonal depression, or a downturn in the economy that could potentially cost us our job. The fall around us can obstruct our lives whether it makes the news or not.

Biblically, we know that "the whole creation has been groaning" (Romans 8:22) with us over these effects. Theologically, we know we have a great high priest who is able "to sympathize with our weaknesses" (Hebrews 4:15). But personally, even when we pray with confidence knowing our pain is fully understood, it can still feel like something is missing. Why is that?

The world continues as if nothing happened. Appointments need to be kept, bills must be paid, errands must be run, and tasks still pile up. So disrespectful! Can't the world push pause for at least forty-eight hours? Who will pay attention to what has happened and stop long enough to honor our hardship? Answer: a friend who has been invited to know us at this depth.

But there's nothing a friend can do about it, we think. We're right. A friend can't unwrite these tragedies from our story.

A friend can't transport us from shock to tranquility. But a friend can give us the gift of presence. A friend can listen enough to "get it." A friend can pause to honor our pain.

A friend often can't make hard times better, but a friend does make hard times less alone. That's powerful. A friend can't erase these moments, but a friend can buffer them. In these moments, the mere presence, awareness, and compassion of a friend is like cartilage that prevents the bone of suffering from rubbing against the bone of isolation. That relief is a wonderful gift that can't be bought, only given.

A FEW QUESTIONS TO ASK

- What tragedies have you experienced in your life?
- What things are not your fault but still negatively impact your life?
- In what moments do you feel alone because you think no one understands or cares?

Chapter 14

WHAT'S HARD? THE FALL WITHIN YOU

DEPTH FOUR

Sometimes, the Genesis 3 impact that is hardest to talk about is not sin. Sometimes it is easier to say, "I was wrong," than, "I have cancer," or, "I have a disability," or, "Trauma has changed me." In these cases, oh, that we could simply repent and move on with life. Comparably, that seems blissful.

Depth four under *what's hard* is when we confide "my life will never be the same" kinds of things. Even if it's as simple as coming to grips with the effects of aging, these can be difficult things to talk about. Topics at this depth feel morbid, depressing, and better to just ignore.

However illogical it is, we often avoid talking about these things because we believe talking about them makes them more real. Our illogical logic says, "If I don't say anything, I can escape into the world of my friend's ignorance. Their lack of awareness means they'll talk to me as if these things weren't real."

But quickly we realize how shallow this approach makes our relationships. Our life is populated with "friends" who know and like us, but we miss the most meaningful benefits of friendship. As our silence persists, we feel the weight of carrying a secret.

Hiding creates a sense of shame. The silence that began as a form of self-protection becomes self-imprisonment.

The key word in this is *shame*. That's a strong word. We likely didn't realize it at first, but in the absence of trusting our closest friends with the hardest parts of our lives, we live as if disclosing these things would make us unacceptable, lesser, undesirable, or marred. That's shame.

If you read literature on shame, even literature that gets into the neuroscience of shame, you'll find that the best remedy is compassionate eye contact from someone who knows your secret.[1] For this reason, a friend is uniquely positioned to assuage shame. The accepting gaze of a friend as they say, "I'm so sorry, but thank you for trusting me enough to tell me," does more than any theological insight or therapeutic technique.

With that in mind, consider Psalm 3. David is on the run for his life. One of his sons staged a coup because David did nothing after another of his sons raped his daughter. David writes this psalm while hiding in a cave hoping his son doesn't find him, realizing his passivity has destroyed his family. David is drowning in a mixture of guilt and shame.

As David prays, notice what he calls God: "the lifter of my head" (v. 3). Remember, shame avoids eye contact. As David bows his head to pray, God realizes this posture reinforces his shame. It is as if God gently reaches his hand under David's chin and lifts David's eyes to meet his. God ministers to David's shame with a loving gaze, not with words or by altering the situation.

Most of us realize that when our friend needs to be heard, we get to be the ambassador of God's ears. And we know that when our friend needs help, we get to be the ambassador of God's hands.

1. If you are interested in reading more about this, consider Curt Thompson, *The Soul of Shame* (Downers Grove, IL: IVP, 2015). In this book, Dr. Thompson explores the experience of shame in multiple dimensions, including its neurophysiology. In his latter chapters, Dr. Thompson focuses on the remedy for shame: vulnerability—being known and seen by good friends who embody God's response to our shame.

But few of us have considered the transformative power that comes when we are an ambassador of God's eyes. We get to be God's eyes to remove the burden of our friend's shame.

As friends, when we're on the caring end of one of these conversations, we might worry, *How do I avoid saying something dumb? How do I not mess it up?* Understanding the power of simple listening and compassionate eye contact gives us the patience to avoid feeling rushed to fill the silence.

Listen, look, smile affirmingly. Say, "Thank you for trusting me enough to share," and wait for your friend to make the next statement.

A FEW QUESTIONS TO ASK

- What experiences in your life or qualities about you lead to a sense of shame?
- What are the non-sin, broken parts of your life you repeatedly ask God to fix?
- When do you feel least known?

Chapter 15

WHAT'S HARD? WHAT YOU'VE NEVER TOLD ANYONE

DEPTH FIVE

As we cross the threshold into hard things we've never told anyone, we are bravely going where we've never allowed a friendship to go before. That's scary, and it's okay to be frightened. My advice is, don't rush it. Just because you're at this point in this book doesn't mean you or one of your friendships is ready for this to be next.

Remember, we're still considering things that are hard but not your fault. Be careful not to confuse the apprehension you may feel with guilt. But because a step like this can be scary, considering a step of this weight requires two types of assessment: the benefit and your readiness.

First, *the benefit* is getting to live without secrets. Secrets haunt and, because of this, secrets isolate. When a friend says, "We need to talk" and you have a secret, what is your instinctive reaction? *Do they know?* Or, you get a compliment but you wonder, *Would they still say that if they knew?*

Secrets hijack pleasant social interactions and turn them into moments of suspense and self-doubt. Let's use the image of a magnet to understand this better. We might think magnets always pull things closer. That's not true. When the same-charged sides of magnets are put close together, they repel one another. This is what happens when we get a compliment from a friend—something we think would draw us closer—but having a secret makes us wonder, *Would they still say that if they knew?* But when you and the friendship are ready, confiding these experiences turns the magnets so they pull the relationship closer together.

Second, there is the question of *your readiness*. Not everything that is good should be next. It may be good to run a marathon, but that doesn't mean I'm ready to embark on a twenty-six-mile jog. The same is true here. Sharing our secrets may be beneficial, but that doesn't mean we're ready.

Several times in this book, we've differentiated friendship from counseling. Here, we'll note how counseling can provide helpful preparation for allowing friendships to develop to this depth. If you are reticent to share your experience with a friend, start with a counselor.

The role of a counselor is to help you process your most difficult experiences. In counseling, *process* is one of those words that sounds clear but is hard to define. In this context, it would mean being able to talk about an experience without being emotionally overwhelmed by it, making peace with the reality that it is part of your story, and being able to regulate your emotions when events remind you of this painful experience.

The role of a friend is different. Talking with a friend helps de-shame an experience. In addition to this, you reclaim parts of your life that had been off-limits with your most trusted friends. When you know you *can* talk about something, you become less preoccupied with that subject coming up when you don't *want* to talk about it. There's a lot of freedom in that.

Remember that you're not trying to build a platoon of depth-thirty-five friendships. Don't feel pressured to fully promote every depth-twenty-five or depth-thirty friendship by sharing this part of your story. You don't owe anyone that. These are inner-circle disclosures. When this is a wise step to take, you are gaining support for something that has been heavy for a long time and you are relinquishing the weight of living with a secret.

Let's reflect on the Bible as a whole again. How many stories are there of hard things that reach depth five? Too many to count. The first human family had one sibling, Cain, who murdered the other, Abel, and had to live with all the fallout that inevitably ensued (Genesis 4). Abram's wife Sarai suffered when her husband cowardly and repeatedly put her in danger, first as they traveled to Egypt and then again with King Abimelech (Genesis 12 and 20). Joseph suffered when his brothers sold him into slavery (Genesis 37). These are Bible heroes, and we've only mentioned a few incidents from the Bible's opening book. The Bible is not naïve about dark secrets.

Why do I bring this up? Sometimes we think the Bible is too pristine to bear the weight of our story. That's not true. There is nothing you will share, when you're ready to share, that the Bible can't handle. Take the time to prepare yourself and let the friendship mature, but don't fear whether God is durable enough to walk faithfully with you amid your story. "Even though I walk through the valley of the shadow of death, I will fear no evil, for you are with me; your rod and your staff, they comfort me" (Psalm 23:4).

A FEW QUESTIONS TO ASK

For this chapter, instead of questions this section provides a few statements you could use to indicate you are available when/if your friend has something weighty to share.

- I appreciate our friendship and want you to know that whatever hard stuff you do (future) or have been through (past), I'm here for you.
- I know there are only a few people anyone goes no-secrets with. I want you to know that I trust you that much.

Summative Exercise 3

SHARING MY UNPOLISHED STORY

This summative exercise is heavier than the first two. In many ways, the question of *what's hard* requires it to be. This depth will often be one of the last we reach.

In this exercise, you'll share the unpolished story of your life, including the hard things, with your closer friends. Before friends can truly appreciate and honor the unpolished parts of our story, they must first know the basic storyline of our life. That is why engaging in this exercise should come after you've done the middle-school-level book exercise from "What's your story?"

> **Question:** Who are the people we would be this vulnerable with?
>
> **Answer:** People who get a vote or voice in major life decisions: a spouse, a mentor, and the friend or friends whose opinion you value most.
>
> **Rationale:** You don't want the people with the most influence in your life exerting that influence with incomplete information.

As we take this step, we realize that one more benefit emerges. We escape the temptation toward *image management*. That's the attempt to control how we are perceived by others. Maybe it's the way we polish our social media accounts to portray a Pollyanna version of our life. Maybe it's the way we frame the stories we tell about ourselves.

Regardless, when we tell those close to us our unpolished story, we are breaking free from image management. To use the imagery from the classic movie *The Wizard of Oz*, once Dorothy saw behind the curtain the wizard lost the ability to be more impressive than he was.

Believe it or not, that's a good thing. Being known by those closest to us for who we truly are—with no fluff, exaggeration, or narrative filtering—is liberating. Being liberated from the pressure to live up to artificially inflated expectations is a blessing, not a curse.

So, what does this summative exercise look like in practice? When we're intentional with developing our friendships, it often happens naturally with our closer friends. As we do life together, they get the skeletal, middle-school-book-review version of our story. This introduces them to the main characters and narrative arc of our life.

Over time they get to know more about the *good*, the *hard*, the *bad*, the *fun*, the *stuck*, and the *what's next* of our life. These details add muscles, tendons, flesh, and pigment to the skeleton of our story. When big things happen or big memories are triggered, we decide whom we will trust with these parts of our story.

It may sound something like this: "You know more of my story than most people. Something happened recently that's a window into the harder part of my story. You've been a good friend and I trust you. Do you have a moment for us to talk about it?"

From there, you fill in the hard part of your story. Depending on the weight of the recent event, sharing your unpolished story can take the relationship to depth three, depth four, or depth five.

Question Four: What's Bad?

Depth One: Your Respectable Sins

Depth Two: Your Most Prevalent Idols

Depth Three: Your Go-To Escapes

Depth Four: Your Code-Orange Sins

Depth Five: Most Likely to Shipwreck Your Life

As we try to understand why it's important to look at *what's bad*, allow me to ask you a silly question that sets up a serious question. If you had to choose whether to wrestle an alligator in a tree or in a swamp, which would you choose? The obvious answer is, in a tree. The nubby little legs and long tail of an alligator give it a profound advantage in a swamp and are an extreme disadvantage in a tree.

Now the serious question: if you had to choose whether to battle your sin in private or in community, which would you choose? The answer is equally obvious, but not as comfortable. We know that trying to battle sin alone is like wrestling an alligator in a swamp, but too often we do it anyway. Borrowing from a famous Bob Newhart counseling skit, the message of this section is, "Stop it! Or Satan will bury you in a swamp!"

My church has a groups-based counseling ministry called G4, which is described in this book's companion resource, *Facilitating Counseling Groups: A Leader's Guide for Group-Based Counseling*

Ministry.[1] In our G4 groups, we have a saying we refer to as a plumb line—a pithy phrase that captures a core value: "You will never be more free than you are honest." Once participants begin to live this way, they love this plumb line. Literally, they have made T-shirts with this slogan on them to wear as jerseys for their group. But initially, honesty is the scariest part of change.

If we want friendship to transform our lives, we must be willing to talk about our sin. We must own the *bad*. The extended version of our G4 plumb line is, "Privacy kills change and fuels sin. Transparency fuels change and kills sin." Transparency may be the most powerful, yet most neglected, tool for character formation.

Like our other questions, we'll take it slow. We'll go deeper one level at a time. Yes, talking about *what's bad* is uncomfortable. But it's also worth it. It's life-changing and liberating.

Another reflection from the counseling office may be helpful even as we're talking about friendship. I periodically hear counselees ask, "Why can't my pastor or friends be as practical as you are?" My reply is, "Have you been as honest with your pastor or friends as you have been with me?"

With anything, from medical visits to home decoration consultations, the more honest and transparent we are about what we want and what's going on, the better the other person can serve us. Withholding pertinent information is the best (meaning the worst) way to muzzle somebody's effectiveness.

Have the courage to continue the journey we've begun. Let's see how God uses your friends to deepen the work he's doing in your life.

---

1. Brad Hambrick and John Chapman, *Facilitating Counseling Groups: A Leader's Guide for Group-Based Counseling Ministry* (Greensboro, NC: New Growth Press, 2023).

Chapter 16

WHAT'S BAD? YOUR RESPECTABLE SINS

DEPTH ONE

Jerry Bridges wrote a book titled *Respectable Sins*.[1] In it, he explores the sins that have become socially acceptable in the church—sins like pride, discontentment, lack of gratitude, and envy.

If your small group discussion asks you to acknowledge a sin struggle, mention one of these and everyone will nod approvingly. You will have been vulnerable enough to fulfill the assignment, vague enough to be in no real danger of changing, and socially savvy enough to avoid making anyone feel uncomfortable. Well done, good and faithful cultural Christian.

Owning *what's bad* at this depth, where you admit respectable sins often, is not much more than a part of how you manage your image. Are these respectable sins bad? Yes. Should we repent of them? Yes. Could you mention most of these in a job interview and still get hired? Also, yes. And if you framed them a certain way, your boss may consider them pros instead of cons.

---

1. Jerry Bridges, *Respectable Sins* (Carol Stream, IL: Tyndale, 2007).

If this kind of acknowledgment is so perfunctory, what good do we gain from depth-one conversations about what's bad? We start to learn the language of honesty and ownership. Recall your first Spanish or French class. You were learning a new language, but you weren't going very deep.

There's no way to get to the advanced classes without it. Even if it's only the equivalent of *comment vous-appelez vous?* ("What is your name?" in French), we need to begin to become fluent at saying things like the following:

- "When I interrupted you, it revealed that I thought what I had to say was more important than what you had to say. That was prideful. Will you forgive me?"
- "My unrest about the level of progress we're making reveals discontentment on my part, not your lack of hard work. Will you forgive me?"
- "You put a lot of effort into that, and I didn't acknowledge it. That's self-preoccupation and a lack of gratitude on my part. Will you forgive me?"

If *comment vous-appelez vous?* is a French 101 sentence, the examples above are What's Bad 101 sentences. They are the basic building blocks for more in-depth conversations.

Now recall how you sounded when you first tried to speak words in a second language. Awkward. Clumsy. I remember being a sophomore in high school and taking French. In front of the class, I had to ask my classmate their name. In my unrefined Kentucky accent I said, "Coma bu a'smella yu?" If I had been trying to be funny, I wouldn't have been as mortified as I was.

The same thing happens as we learn the new language of candor about our sin. At first, it sounds clunky and forced. How do we fix that? The same way I added some ooh-la-la to my country boy dialect: practice.

Don't be discouraged by your need to practice. From Genesis 3 on, the native tongue of the human heart has been blame-shifting, minimizing, and willful blindness. From God's first post-sin question to Adam and Eve, "Where are you?" (Genesis 3:9), he's been inviting us to acknowledge what is already obvious. Like any journey, you start where you are and take the next step. Be depth-one honest about your respectable sins with people to whom you've bestowed the title of friend.

A FEW QUESTIONS TO ASK

- When and where do you struggle with the sins of pride, ingratitude, or people-pleasing?
- How difficult is it for you to acknowledge these sins after they occur?
- Whom do you admire that owns their faults well?

Chapter 17

WHAT'S BAD? YOUR MOST PREVALENT IDOLS

DEPTH TWO

This may be the rare occasion when depth two may not feel more vulnerable than depth one. Here, we're going to consider the *good things that compel us to do bad things*. Most of us don't do bad things for bad reasons. We want something good, and we cross a few lines as we pursue it.

The Bible calls the good things behind the bad things we do idols. People aren't that complicated. We do what we do to get what we want. Whatever this thing is becomes an idol when we're willing to sin to get it. In that moment, we are loving it more than we love God.

What are common idols? Things like respect, appreciation, comfort, image, peace, justice, unity, pleasure, achievement, or affirmation. Notice that all these things really are good. Let's take a common response to a common sin and insert a few of these words: "I'm sorry I lost my cool, but I was just trying to be a good father (image) and make everybody happy (peace and unity) by figuring out what we were going to do, but no one seemed to care (appreciation)."

If you've ever tried to lead a group of people, you can relate. But these good things pushed this father to lose his cool, however harsh that may have been. In light of this, read James 4:1–2: "What causes quarrels and what causes fights among you? Is it not this, that your *passions* are at war within you? You desire and do not have, so you murder. You covet and cannot obtain, so you fight and quarrel" (emphasis added).

Why did I emphasize the word *passions*? In context, most of us would think this was a bad word. But James didn't use the Greek word for lust here. He used the neutral word that we would use to describe how we feel about our work, hobbies, and faith—our passions. In effect, James is saying, "You wanted good things, you didn't get them, so those good things compelled you to do bad things."

Notice, James isn't making a "well, your heart was in the right place" appeal. James is not making excuses; he is calling these Christians to identify and own the motives behind their sin—that is, their idols. This is what good friends do. Friends don't let friends excuse sin just because they have decent motives.

The great thing about motives is that they are usually pretty consistent. Identify your top three idols and you've probably found the root of 90 percent of your sin. What's most important to you doesn't fluctuate that much.

Here's the principle: *we tend to hear or see first what we fear most*. As a kid, I liked to take my BB gun and dog traipsing through the woods to "hunt" (for what, I don't know). The problem was, I had a fear of snakes. Because of that, every crooked stick was a snake until it proved otherwise.

As grownups, we do the same thing. Do you idolize respect? Chances are every comment that doesn't align with your agenda flashes as disrespect until proven otherwise. Do you idolize appreciation? Then it's likely you perceive more people taking you for granted than actually are. What we see often reveals more about us than it does the other person. Because of our sin nature, we are prone to interpret the actions of others through the lens of our idols. The more we are honest with our friends about our idols, the greater freedom from them we can begin to experience.

A FEW QUESTIONS TO ASK

- When you do something bad, what are the most common good things you're focused on?
- What themes do you see or hear first when you're upset with others?
- What are your top three idols? What percentage of your sins do you think these idols account for?

Chapter 18
WHAT'S BAD? YOUR GO-TO ESCAPES
DEPTH THREE

Here's the great thing, in the sinister sense, about sin: it's never too busy and it always understands. It will always meet you where you are and take you further than you want to go. Sin is the best bad friend you've ever had.

If you want to identify where trouble is going to come from, look for early warning-sign answers to these sentence-completion exercises:

- After a long day, I...
- When I feel misunderstood, I...
- When I disappoint myself, I...
- When a conflict goes poorly, I...
- When I'm bored, I...

Our go-to escapes might seem innocent enough at first glance, but they should be seen as early warning signs, a code yellow, so to speak. Maybe some of the answers you came up with during the sentence-completion exercise seem "not that dangerous" to you: self-pity, drinking alone, mindless internet browsing, isolation, escaping through food, or the like. These may not seem like ruinous, code-red sins, but, left unconfided and unchecked, they still have the potential to undermine your life.

Chances are that these go-to escapes are things you either haven't told your friends about or have strongly minimized. Ask yourself why you haven't said more about these things to the people you supposedly trust.

As an aside, if you reward yourself in good times with the same thing you comfort yourself with in hard times, the propensity for these bad things to destroy your life increases significantly.

As an honest question (not a gotcha question), ask yourself, "What would I lose if I gave up my go-to escape?" Chances are the answer is some version of "the ability to cope with hard times." Do you see what these go-to escapes are? They are friend replacements and God replacements. These escapes are filling the roles that God and good friends fill in a healthy life.

How do you get all the air out of a bottle? Fill it with water or sand. What happens when we fill the pivotal moments of our life with these escapes? We crowd God and good friends out of those moments. That's a double danger: the presence of the escaping behavior, and the absence of redemptive influences. What does it take to reverse this? Courage. The courage to be honest with our friends.

Think of the protection these escapes provide like the protection given when a child hides under the bed. Is the child safer under the bed? No, there's just a façade of safety. But to come out from under the bed requires double courage for the child: the courage to forsake their faux protection and the courage to face whatever prompted them to go under the bed.

That is what is being asked of you—double courage. Forsake your escape and embrace God's design for responding to these unpleasant situations. Your go-to escape will never walk with you toward God like a good friend will.

A FEW QUESTIONS TO ASK

- When something bothers you, what are the healthy and unhealthy ways you seek comfort?
- What would be the best ways for me to encourage you during these times?
- What are the things you most fear I would say if you reached out to me during these times?

Chapter 19

WHAT'S BAD? YOUR CODE-ORANGE SINS

DEPTH FOUR

"I may (code-yellow sin), but I won't (code-orange sin)."

How do you fill in the blanks? What are the lesser sins you excuse (yellow) and the moderate sins that at this point still aggravate your conscience (orange), as you're on the way to the life-altering sins you say you'll never commit (red)?

"I may speed, but not more than seven miles per hour over the limit," doesn't count. Maybe, "I may flirt, but I won't have an emotional affair, much less cheat on my spouse." Perhaps you're playing the emerging addict game: "It's not a problem as long as I don't start drinking before noon."

What sin have you created a line for that you won't cross? Where did your line start? How many times have you moved your line? When you start making deals with yourself, it's a strong indication you need to phone a friend.

Realize that a prerequisite for being honest with a friend is being honest with yourself. If you believe your own lies, you won't feel like you're lying when you say deceptive things to others. So, honestly, if this line keeps moving in the direction it's going, at the rate it's moving, where does it end up?

Now comes **the big choice**: *choose pre-crisis honesty with a trusted friend over post-crisis honesty with everyone who sees your crisis!* As a counselor, I can testify that the vast majority of really messy things that get discussed in my office could have been resolved with "just a friend" if the person were willing to be honest during the code-yellow or code-orange phase.

Think of sin in your life like termites in your home. When you notice that little ant with wings, you may tap the wall with your fist and think, *It's still solid enough. Nothing to worry about*. Even if the first statement is true, the second statement is foolish. If you call the exterminator now, it may cost you a little. If you wait until it can't be avoided, it will cost much more. That's the gamble we take with hidden sin.

Consider Proverbs 28:13, "Whoever conceals his transgressions will not prosper, but he who confesses and forsakes them will obtain mercy." You may feel like you've been proving the first part of this verse wrong for a while. Maybe your code-orange sin is financial, and you are still prospering. But like any coach whose team is trailing says, the game is not over.

You might ask, "Does 'obtaining mercy' mean that if I confess the consequences will be less?" I can't promise that. Maybe. But if you are more worried about consequences of sin than freedom from sin, you're still playing games. The reason you talk to a friend is because you want freedom, not a plea bargain. Don't go for cut-rate termite extermination. Make sure you remove the threat.

This chapter is modeled after the approach to sin Jesus teaches in Matthew 5:21–30. Jesus traces the "big sins" of murder and adultery back to the heart sins of anger and lust. Jesus urges us to take sin seriously early in its development and to take any means necessary to ensure the job is done right: "If your right eye causes you to sin, tear it out and throw it away. For it is better that you lose one of your members than that your whole body be thrown into hell" (v. 29). In response to this chapter, "surgery" means as you put down this book, pick up your phone, and call a friend.

A FEW QUESTIONS TO ASK

- Don't make your friend ask the "magic question," knowing what to ask without you confiding your struggle. Just be honest.
- What do you need to tell me that you haven't?

Chapter 20

WHAT'S BAD?

MOST LIKELY TO SHIPWRECK YOUR LIFE

DEPTH FIVE

When *suffering* derails our life, it usually catches us by surprise. We didn't see the medical diagnosis coming. We had no idea we would lose our house to a fire. We didn't expect our trusted friend or spouse to betray us.

But when *sin* shipwrecks our life, it rarely catches us off guard. We know when we're pushing the limits financially, so we shouldn't be surprised when we get busted for a shady business deal. We know we're escaping through substances, so we shouldn't be surprised when the repercussions of addiction set in. If we're honest enough to admit it, we know.

It's not just that we know as we're doing it. If we give it any forethought, we know what temptations are most likely to be our demise. There's a decent chance we could have answered this question by the time we graduated high school. If a sin was going to shipwreck your life, what would it be?

It doesn't take the spiritual gift of prophecy to answer this question. It takes the character trait of courage. It doesn't require divine insight; it takes the willingness to look at our life and be honest.

Did Moses know anger was likely to be his downfall? He should have. It was a theme of his life long before he let loose with a tirade that resulted in God removing him as the leader who would bring Israel into the promised land (Numbers 20). Earlier in his life, Moses had killed an Egyptian for beating one of his people (Exodus 2). Moses had angrily smashed the Ten Commandments tablets after finding the people worshiping the golden calf, and he punished them by making them drink their ground-up idol (Exodus 32). An honest Moses wouldn't have excused this emerging pattern just because others were at fault too.

Talking to a friend isn't a foolproof solution to avoiding the pitfall of our characteristic temptations. But I don't think it's a coincidence that Moses's demise came after his bond with his closest confidants, Aaron and Miriam, was damaged (Numbers 12). When Moses went from supported to isolated, it didn't take long for his besetting sin to ruin his life.

The question for you is, have you started as well as Moses started? Moses knew the importance of having good friends for accountability and support; that's why you see Aaron and Miriam mentioned early and often in Moses's life. When Moses was at his spiritual best, it is clear he was being honest and vulnerable with these trusted friends. As you identify your closest friends, who are the ones you need to have a *what's wrong* depth-five conversation with? Pick one or two and make the call. The heartache you'll never know because you did will make it well worth it.

A FEW QUESTIONS TO ASK

- If a sin was going to shipwreck your life, what would it be?
- Is there any present reason for concern?
- What are the best ways and times for me to check in on you?

Summative Exercise 4

"NOT THAT BAD" PHONE CALLS

This summative exercise is pretty simple, but not easy. To help you see the significance of this exercise, I will invite you into a common first counseling session dialogue.

> Counselor: "You've struggled with this for a while. Why pursue counseling now?"
>
> Counselee: "Well, I guess until recently, it didn't seem *that bad*."

This phenomenon is not unique to counseling. Talk to any pain specialist, mechanic, or nutritionist and you'll hear the same story: "I wish my clients didn't wait until their car, joints, pain, eating disorder, or ______ symptom got *that bad* before they called me."

The rationale is the same for all of them: it would cost the client less, they would benefit more, and their life would be better if they called sooner. But we don't.

What does this mean? It means you've been bartering with yourself for the last three chapters. You made it through sharing your respectable sins and motives decently well. But as we turned the corner toward your go-to escapes, you started to hedge. You're not necessarily against the latter three chapters, you just haven't done anything with them yet. After all, things aren't *that bad*.

This is the watershed decision that determines if the *what's bad* question does any good. If you wait until things get *that bad*, it won't. At that point, this question will only magnify pain by regret. But if you get in the habit of making a call while things are still "not that bad," you'll never know how much pain you've avoided. Those painful chapters of your life story will go unwritten.

So, what is a "not that bad" phone call? It's the phone call you make before an emergency. It's the phone call that helps prevent the emergency in the first place. Don't wait. Glean the personal insights you harvested from the previous three chapters and call a friend to say, "Things aren't *that bad*, but I've been reading a book on friendship. It says we should talk." From there, use the questions at the end of each chapter as a conversation prompt. Repeat whenever there is a moral code yellow.

Again, this isn't complicated. But it is life-changing.

Notice that *what's bad?* is only one of seven questions. That means this question won't morph friendships into sin-hunt relationships. That's a false fear. Relationships based only on keeping someone accountable for their sin tend to fade, because the time spent together becomes redundant and negative. But engaging our other six questions makes for a true friendship full of vitality, positivity, creativity, and fun.

Don't let your closest friendship be a six-question friendship, where you talk about everything but what's bad. If you do, you will end up like sailors in the era of sea exploration, who suffered from inadequate nutrition due to limited variety in their food rations.

These sailors were convinced they had packed enough food for their journeys. By calorie count, they were right. But a greater number of sea explorers died of malnutrition than died in every major war in modern history. Why? They had everything they needed except vitamin C, so they got scurvy. The answer was simple: pack some lemons.

Packing lemons is no harder than calling a friend, and it can be equally lifesaving. Maybe you can sip lemonade while you talk about what's bad.

Question Five: What's Fun?

Depth One: What Brings You Joy

Depth Two: Why You Enjoy These Things

Depth Three: Can I Try It Too?

Depth Four: Sacrificing for Your Joys

Depth Five: Feeling Your Joys

After two heavy questions about *what's hard* and *what's bad*, we need a break. Amen? Amen! All right, let's ask *what's fun*.

Fun is the soil from which most friendships initially grow. We have a common interest, so we're in the same place at the same time, multiple times, and conversations flow naturally. Before you know it, we've laughed and almost accidentally gleaned most of the depth-one and depth-two information from the other six questions.

But fun is more than the jumper cables of friendship. Yes, fun can just be surface-level bonding. But fun, like our other roots, can also be a vital part of taking friendship to deeper depths.

The things that bring us joy provide a unique window into our lives. We are usually the most transparent in our joy. We are free with our words, genuine with our emotions, and expressive with our faces. This makes it easier to get to know each other around *what's fun* than some of our other questions.

But *what's fun* still requires intentionality if we want to prevent friendships from stalling out. The distraction of joy can be a reason that friendships don't grow deeper. Compare these two statements.

1. I delight in what you delight in.
2. I delight in your delight.

The first statement indicates an *enjoyable acquaintance*. The second statement marks something that has the potential to be a *transformative friendship*. Both are good. Enjoyable acquaintances are a blessing. But in this book, we are cultivating something more meaningful.

For me, the contrast is more clearly seen in the difference between my grandfather, "Namps," and my mother. Both faithfully came to my Little League baseball games. Namps came because he loved baseball—and me. With every strike I threw, he exclaimed, "That's a Cracker Jack!" (I don't know why he said that. It was just his thing.) My mother, who still barely knows the rules of the game, came only because she loved me.

I appreciated both of them, and Namps bought better post-game snacks when I did well. Namps and I shared a common joy. But my mom enjoyed *my* joy. As we deepen relationships through *what's fun*, we don't want to limit ourselves to people with common interests. We want to build selfless friendships where each other's joy means more than the activity. Toward that goal, we'll once more grow deeper one step at a time.

Chapter 21

WHAT'S FUN? WHAT BRINGS YOU JOY

DEPTH ONE

Joy is usually obvious. You can hear it in someone's voice. You can see it on their face: "A glad heart makes a cheerful face" (Proverbs 15:13). About the only time we try to hide our joy is with our first crush when we want to play it cool instead of being transparent about how much we like them.

With *what's fun* depth one, the instructions are simple: you do you, and pay attention to who's around as you do. For me, this looks like Little League coaching. I coached every team our boys played on until they started high school ball.

My favorite ages to coach are eight- to ten-year-olds. At these ages, kids are cognitively and physically able to implement instruction and grasp team concepts. But they aren't yet teenagers, so they don't cop an attitude with you.

Every week they do something they didn't think was possible. They are innocent enough that their enthusiasm glows all over their faces. Put a little eye black on their cheeks and they think they are in William Wallace's army getting ready to defend all of Scotland every Tuesday night.

I hope you are smiling as you read that, even if you're not a baseball person. At depth one, *what's fun* is about smiling, laughing, and listening. Did you notice the verbs? Smile. Laugh. Listen.

Those are the skills we need for the early part of our journey. Whatever it is that you enjoy doing, smile as you do it. Listen to those who are around you. Give yourself to the moment enough to laugh. Be fully present *in* the moment and *with* the people around you. For too many of us, *what's fun* is the only time we slow down enough to be fully in the moment and with people.

As you do this, what is happening? You are getting to know people. You are building casual relationships that can become meaningful friendships. As I coached, I got to know a lot about a lot of people. Players, families, other coaches, and even an umpire or two became friends.

I got to know people's **story**. I learned why a family moved from California to North Carolina. I learned about a family's decision to adopt.

I got to know what was **good**. I got to affirm players who worked hard, whether they were the most talented or not. I got to affirm older siblings who were willing to help run practice.

I got to know what was **hard**. I got to help young athletes learn how to respond to making an error or going into a slump. I got to talk with players trying to figure out how to respond to their parents' divorce.

I got to know what was **bad**. I heard dads say, "I know I need to be less hard on my son." I got to support parents when they had a player sit out a game for neglecting their schoolwork.

Fun is a doorway to lots of other questions. Walk through that door. Enjoy it. Engage with people. Use the rest of this book to intentionally avoid allowing these new relationships to stall out as casual acquaintances. Keep your eyes open for those relationships that can shape and enrich your life for years to come.

A FEW QUESTIONS TO ASK

- When you get a day off, what's your favorite thing to do?
- What was your favorite thing to do as a kid?
- What are the most life-giving things you've done this month?

Chapter 22

WHAT'S FUN? WHY YOU ENJOY THESE THINGS

DEPTH TWO

The journey from *what* to *why* deepens a friendship. In the last chapter, I told you *what* I enjoyed: coaching. In this chapter, I'll tell you *why*.

Our joys are biographical; they emerge from our life stories. I grew up in a small town without any coaches who knew how to teach the fundamentals of baseball. I worked hard because I loved the game, and I managed to walk on to a college baseball team. In college, I finally learned how to play baseball correctly just as I began competing beyond my talent level.

That's why I enjoy helping young athletes maximize their talent with good fundamentals early. The beaming, I-can't-believe-I-really-did-that smile of a young athlete is my drug of choice.

When you help someone do something they didn't think possible, it gives you a profound influence on their life. Helping athletes navigate disappointment, maintain higher priorities as they pursue their athletic goals, and respond to success with humility are lessons that will benefit every area of life for the rest of their lives.

Coaching also provides me with a change of pace. Most of my day is spent managing crises, writing, teaching, and consulting.

These are indoor activities that are cognitively and emotionally taxing. Coaching happens outdoors and is focused on reaching goals and pursuing dreams.

That's the *why* behind my joy of coaching. How about you? *Why* do you enjoy *what* you enjoy?

If our friendships are going to grow deeper than sharing mutually enjoyable activities, we can't be mindless about our joys. We'll need to reflect on the things we enjoy.

Proverbs 20:5 says, "The purpose in a man's heart is like deep water, but a man of understanding will draw it out." As we go deeper with each of our seven questions, this is what we are doing. We are delving into the deeper waters of each other's joys.

In your friendships, play this game: connect the fun moment with one of the other questions. For instance, this is what you might say to me after a game or practice.

- **Connect with *story*:** Smile and say, "These kids won't have to unlearn as many bad habits as we did."
- **Connect with *what's good*:** "It was great watching Stephen get his first hit. I think you enjoyed it as much as he did. I appreciate how you invest in these kids."
- **Connect with *what's hard*:** "I can tell you're sad that the Wilson family pulled their son off the team. You can't make everyone happy, but I think everyone knows how much you care."
- **Connect with *what's bad*:** "I think you're starting to want success for Jimmy more than he wants it for himself. That may be why you're pushing him too hard."

The first two are forms of encouragement. The third is a mixture of comfort and encouragement. The last one is a word of caution about how passion may devolve into sin. Shared joy provides an entry point for these kinds of conversations. Simple statements like these are the pivot points where casual acquaintances begin to mature into transformative friendships.

A FEW QUESTIONS TO ASK

- When did you start to enjoy ______?
- What's the most rewarding or satisfying part of ______ for you?
- What makes ______ an emotional net win for you?

Chapter 23

WHAT'S FUN? CAN I TRY IT TOO?

DEPTH THREE

My wife likes football more than baseball; she's a football coach's daughter. She likes antiques more than coaching tools; she's a history teacher specializing in World War II. She cross-stitches while we watch the evening news. She owns more power tools than I do because she enjoys refurbishing antique furniture.

Another friend, Jonathan, warned me early on, "I don't like sportsball." Instead of athletics, he likes writing, cooking, and good conversations. He has daughters while I have sons, so our familial extracurricular interests don't overlap at all. We grew up differently and in different parts of the country.

But although our interests diverge, an important part of my relationships with my wife and with Jonathan is *can I try it too?* This is about curiosity, other-minded joy, and generosity of time. *Can I try it too?* shouldn't be reduced to mutual participation.

Think of a grandmother whose grandson loves to surf the giant waves off the shores of French Polynesia. She's probably not waxing her own board and waiting to catch the next mammoth white crest. That would be one gnarly grandma. But what does she do? She asks curious questions, delights in his stories, and fixes his favorite dinner so there is plenty of time to talk about his day.

We can all do a version of that with any joy our friends might delight in. I ask Sallie where she got her latest cross-stitching pattern, whom she's making it for, why she chose it, and how she plans to gift it. I ask Jonathan about what he cooked recently, whom he cooked it for, where he got the recipe, and how he thinks it turned out.

This idea is a simple application of the second great commandment, "You shall love your neighbor as yourself" (Mark 12:31). Loving our neighbor as ourselves involves, at least in part, delighting in what they delight in.

If we look for natural overlap in our joys, it's rather easy to reach this depth. Although I don't cross-stitch, I do like quiet evenings at home, so Sallie and I enjoy that time together for different reasons. And although Jonathan has daughters and I have sons, we both value being good dads. We can each be intrigued by learning from how the other is investing in their family.

Paul would frequently embrace the preferences of others to love them. He went so far as to say:

> To the Jews I became as a Jew, in order to win Jews. To those under the law I became as one under the law (though not being myself under the law) that I might win those under the law. To those outside the law I became as one outside the law (not being outside the law of God but under the law of Christ) that I might win those outside the law. To the weak I became weak, that I might win the weak. I have become all things to all people, that by all means I might save some. (1 Corinthians 9:20–22)

If Paul adjusted his preferences on these weightier matters to connect with others, surely he did the same for mundane enjoyments to deepen relationships. We can imagine that to those who loved soccer, Paul became a fan of soccer to forge a better relationship. For those who strummed a lyre (an ancient precursor to the modern guitar), Paul listened to their latest songs to learn what was meaningful to them. For those who like to read, Paul asked about their favorite authors (literally, see Acts 17:28). A large chunk of the New Testament is Paul writing to many of these casual acquaintances who had become dear friends. Romans 16 is an entire chapter devoted to listing and affirming these friends.

If you want the number of friends in your life that Paul lists, invest in friendships like Paul did. Be curious about the things other people enjoy. If possible, engage what they enjoy with them. If not, still be willing to learn and to be generous with your time as you listen.

When it comes time to navigate the deeper levels of *what's hard*, *what's bad*, and *what's stuck* in each other's lives, the time you invested in depth-three fun will have garnered the relational capital to allow you to explore more difficult things. The stories and laughter you shared will have cultivated the trust to be heard and the awareness to know what to say in those life-shaping moments. It begins with how we steward our joys.

A FEW QUESTIONS TO ASK

- How long have you done ______?
- Do you mind if I join you sometime when you're doing ______?
- Can we get lunch? I'd love to hear more about ______.

Chapter 24

WHAT'S FUN? SACRIFICING FOR YOUR JOYS

DEPTH FOUR

Are you ready to take a big jump again? Depth three was just about showing interest in things that aren't naturally compelling for you. But with depth four, we move from the *selfless* practice of "Love your neighbor as yourself" to the *self-denial* of "Let him deny himself and take up his cross daily" (Luke 9:23). Even if we don't naturally enjoy the things that bring joy to our closest friends, we invest *sacrificially* with our time and energy in the things that bring them joy. We learn to find joy in their joy as we do.

Being selfless and self-denial are both biblical virtues. But self-denial is something we embrace for more meaningful relationships. The reality is that meaningful friendships, the kind that transform our lives, will cost us something. This is true with each question we explore, even *what's fun*.

For me, self-denial might mean giving up the rare breaks I get from drama. As a counselor, I live a drama-saturated life infused with hardships and crises. Tissues are a larger-than-expected part of my business expense. Because I'm a counselor, when someone says to me, "I've been meaning to ask you . . . ," the rest of the sentence is usually on the deep end of *what's bad* or *what's hard*.

Even my casual acquaintances navigate toward heavier topics. When people learn I'm a counselor, they seek advice more than conversation. This happens with professions other than counselors: attorneys, doctors, social workers, and sometimes even pastors. Be mindful of this when you have friends in these professions. It's not friendship when you are asking questions because of someone's credentials and training instead of your tenure of relationship and mutual respect.

But with my closer friends, their questions are the fruit of our friendship. There is a degree of satisfaction ("fun" in pastel rather than neon) in serving a friend, even when conversations delve into areas I would normally redirect to formal counseling with people I do not know as well.

What is the equivalent for you? Maybe it's not related to your vocation. But what do you avoid for legitimate reasons in casual relationships that you need to allow in your closest friendships, so that they aren't hampered from growing deeper? This would be a place to practice self-denial.

One way to identify the answer to this question is to consider which of the depth-four or depth-five recommendations for the other six questions unsettle you. Don't shut down and think, *Well, that's why I don't have closer friends*. Reflect on why that action is uncomfortable. Consider sharing it with one of your closer friends as a *what's hard* conversation. Look for opportunities to engage that aspect of friendship in a pastel-fun type of enjoyment—enjoyable because it enriches a valued relationship rather than because it is what you would have chosen otherwise.

In time, this actually can turn into a deeply satisfying kind of fun. Reflect on some of the hardest things you've done in your life. Think about the people who were part of those achievements. When you talk with those people about those accomplishments, how do you feel? The answer is usually that you feel joyful in a deeply fulfilled sense. What started as a pastel, subdued, sacrificial form of joy may not have turned into an excited-neon joy, but it does become a darker, richer version of that joy.

That is the nature of depth-four *what's fun* activities. They may be far from your first choice for that moment, but they're worth it because they forge such meaningful bonds between friends. When we look back on these sacrificial joys, we realize they cemented some of our most valued friendships.

A FEW QUESTIONS TO ASK

- What are your neon joys? What are your pastel joys?
- What are the hardest things you've done that you didn't enjoy at the time, but now take great satisfaction in?
- What things do you do well in other areas of life that you prefer to avoid in your casual friendships?

Chapter 25

WHAT'S FUN? I FEEL YOUR JOYS

DEPTH FIVE

Feeling a friend's joys is like other depth-five markers. Trying to engage at this depth before a friendship has had time to mature feels intrusive or forced. When we hit depth five on any question, we're hitting a sphere that we only share with a few people, even on the fun stuff.

In a nonsexual way, friendship is intimate. When someone knows you well enough to delight in your joys as their own, you realize how close that relationship is. This depth of knowing each other results in a profound influence on each other's lives. That realization is both encouraging and intimidating.

Imagine friends of all depths attending a major life event, like a graduation or wedding. Everyone is sharing a depth-two kind of moment. They recognize the achievement, appreciate the life marker, and echo the smile on your face.

But there are a few people who know you at a deeper level. You can see their joy isn't just a reflection of your joy, like a mirror. Their joy is harmonizing with your joy like a song. Maybe you would say they "get it" or they're invested in this moment. Whatever you call it, you sense their connection to this moment is qualitatively deeper.

When these people say congratulations, they mean more than most people using the same word. They share your joy within a depth-five understanding of your story. They know the depth-five hardships you navigated to arrive at this point. Their "well done" statement isn't about the moment, but about the journey. They were a companion on the journey, not just a fan at the finish line.

In this, we see the interrelatedness of our seven questions. Going deeper on one question increases the significance of all the others. As a friendship deepens, everything about that friendship becomes more meaningful.

Via this book, we are creating our own Hebrews 12 "cloud of witnesses" (v. 1). These are people whose deep devotion to Christ is bearing fruit in our life as their example challenges us to grow, and vice versa. In these friendships, we "lay aside" sin and lesser things to "run with endurance the race that is set before us" (v. 1). Meaningful friendship is a form of training; it is about pursuing something together.

Whether you have played on a sports team or performed in an orchestra or recital, you know this effect. Together, you sacrificed things (i.e., lay aside) for a shared joy and objective. When the pivotal moment came, the intuitive celebration was not, "*I* did it!" but "*We* did it!" This is the cloud-of-witnesses-effect. *Me* melts into the *we* in a way that deepens our joy because it is shared.

As athletes celebrate a victory, a ballet team celebrates a recital, or a staff team celebrates reaching a major goal, "I feel your joy" infuses these moments with greater significance. Decades later, when these depth-five friends see one another, they'll say, "Do you remember when…?" and savor afresh their accomplishment. Shared joy makes time evaporate; we feel like "it was only yesterday."

Whenever you get to a pivotal moment of life, and the moment is elevated because a "you were part of me getting to this moment" friend is there, *What's fun* depth five is occurring. In these moments, we realize all the sacrifices were worth it because this moment would be incomplete without the presence of these friends.

A FEW QUESTIONS TO ASK

- When you graduated high school, what was the most meaningful conversation you had and who was it with? Pick any comparable life event.
- Has there been a major life event that felt "less than" because you didn't have a quality friend to share it with?
- When it comes to commemorating and celebrating a major life event or achievement, what is the most meaningful way someone can share that moment with you?

Summative Exercise 5

SKILLFULLY BLESSING SOMEONE WITH THEIR JOYS

This summative exercise is the action-focused mirror of the verbally focused exercise for *what's good*. With that exercise, you were asked to engage in a perpetual scavenger hunt seeking things in your friends to affirm—using words. With this exercise, we're going to engage in a scavenger hunt looking for opportunities to bless our friends with what they enjoy—using actions. You will skillfully bless them with their joys.

The term *skillfully* is chosen for a purpose. It is a depth-dependent term. For instance, what it means to be a skilled debater changes depending on whether a person is six years old, sixteen, or twenty-six. At six, it means you can con Mom and Dad into delaying bedtime. By sixteen, it might mean talking your way out of a speeding ticket. And by twenty-six, it would mean using advanced oratory skills in your vocation.

As you think about skillfully blessing your friends, be content to do so at the depth of each friendship.

I remember the best piece of parenting advice I received as Sallie and I awaited our first child. A mentor said to me, "Don't get caught looking to the next season of life." When your son is toddling, don't get caught daydreaming about what he will do when he can run. Enjoy that moment for what it has to offer.

The same principle applies to friendship. Don't get caught up wishing each friendship was a little deeper. Enjoy it for where it is. Intentionally investing in each friendship at its current depth is the best way to nurture that friendship to a deeper level.

- With a **depth-one fun friend**, bring a gift to your next shared activity that allows them to enjoy it a bit more.
- With a **depth-two fun friend**, remember a story about why they began to enjoy that activity and comment on it to show you value the relationship.
- With a **depth-three fun friend**, engage something they enjoy that's not a primary joy for you. If they enjoy something you wouldn't do together, ask about it and enjoy the conversation.
- With a **depth-four fun friend**, participate in something you don't enjoy for the benefit of the friendship. Take satisfaction (pastel joy) in how it blesses your friend.
- With a **depth-five fun friend**, look for those pivotal moments that serve as life markers and find ways for your shared history together to accentuate the moment.

From depth one to depth five, we can *skillfully* bless our friends with their joys. Most of the time, maybe with the exception of depth four, this merely involves doing what you would do anyway with greater intentionality.

In that sense, this summative exercise is a lighthearted application of Philippians 2:4, "Let each of you look not only to his own interests, but also to the interests of others." As you do the things you enjoy, don't *only* focus on what you enjoy. Look also for ways to deepen your friendship by being thoughtful about how and why they enjoy it too.

Question Six: What's Stuck?

Depth One: When Your Ruts Were Life-Giving

Depth Two: When the Color Began to Fade

Depth Three: When Guilt and Duty Took Over

Depth Four: How You're Stuck in Stubbornness

Depth Five: How You're Stuck in Shame

I grew up on a farm, so I'm an expert on ruts. Ruts are the product of repetition, traversing the same terrain in the same way over and over and over again. In a literal sense, it means the same pickup truck taking the same dirt road for decades. For this section about *what's stuck*, we'll consider the metaphorical ruts of mindless habits and faded pleasures.

The first thing we should note about ruts is that they come from what's good. Habits start because they accomplish something helpful; otherwise we wouldn't repeat them. Some habits are trivial, like our morning routine. Other habits have profound consequences, like a doctor following presurgical protocols.

Human life is better because of our ability to habituate multifaceted tasks. We would be cognitively exhausted if we couldn't habituate.

But ruts are habits drained of life, like faded drapes exposed to the sun for too long. When this happens, good habits provide an ever-diminishing return. We've identified a rut when we realize something that used to give life now only makes us feel guilty or "off" if we omit it. But the incremental loss of enjoyment is often small enough we don't notice it happening.

If you eat the same breakfast every day for three years, at first you may love it, but eventually it's just what you do. Most Christians have experienced this with their daily Bible reading time. They find an approach they love. They do it. They keep doing it. Eventually, they find they aren't getting as much from a spiritual discipline that has faded into a lifeless routine.

Ruts are excellent passageways into transformative friendships. Our ruts were initially part of *what's good*. We repeated them for so long they became part of *what's your story*. As they faded, they likely became part of *what's hard*. If our life is going to improve, then our *what's stuck* must be revitalized. Friendships are the most natural place to talk about changes at this mundane level.

Our goal in the chapters ahead is to help you and your friends become good rut archaeologists. You'll examine old ruts like Aztec ruins, recalling what life was like when these ruts were fresh and life-giving. But like a good historian, you won't study history for history's sake. You'll study history to glean from it lessons that enhance the present.

Think of it this way: exploring habits is like an expedition through your grandparents' attic. I remember doing this as a child. I can smell the mothballs and mildew as I opened my grandfather's World War II travel chest, picking up old maps, finding a tool and wondering what it was for.

By doing this alongside faithful friends, you will get to know each other better and become agents of change in each other's lives. Few things impact us as pervasively as breathing life into once-meaningful habits and reclaiming what made them good. Let's go!

Chapter 26

WHAT'S STUCK? WHEN YOUR RUTS WERE LIFE-GIVING

DEPTH ONE

The earliest depth in sharing about ruts with a friend is to reminisce about when those ruts were life-giving. We all love sharing stories from the good ol' days.

Let's pick up the example of a daily Bible reading time. Maybe you were like me. As a new Christian, I opened my Bible and read whatever chapter my Bible opened to. That was life-giving *for a while*. Then it felt random.

So, then I read through one book at a time. For a while, that was life-giving. Eventually, it felt too much like English class. Next, I found a read-the-Bible-in-a-year plan. A new approach brought new life to this habit, but eventually that became stale too. Then I printed a book of the Bible on computer paper, double-spaced and with wide margins so I could make notes. You know where the story goes from here.

Remember, at this depth we're not judging ruts, we're celebrating them. We're asking what *was* good about what's *now* stuck. There was a season when each Bible reading approach was life-giving. One of the great tricks to life is finding ways to stay engaged with life-giving practices without allowing their nourishment to fade through routine.

Look at each area of your life. What are your habits?

- **Daily:** Morning, afternoon, and evening routines
- **Relational:** Friends, family, and conversation routines
- **Faith:** Spiritual discipline routines
- **Physical:** Exercise, eating, and sleeping routines
- **Off time:** Recreational, hobby, and fun routines
- **Logistical:** Financial and scheduling routines

Now consider how each of these routines are (or were) life-giving.

- What do you enjoy about each one?
- How does each habit/rut make life more efficient or effective?
- How does each habit/rut grow you as a person?
- How does each habit/rut make your life or relationships richer?

First Corinthians 13:11 is a lens through which you can view your habits that have lost their luster: "When I was a child, I spoke like a child, I thought like a child, I reasoned like a child. When I became a man, I gave up childish ways." Too often, we view this verse negatively.

Is it bad for a child to think, talk, and play like a child? Not at all. How does an adult feel when they dig through their childhood closet and find old toys? Not guilty, but nostalgic. They smile as they rekindle memories with their favorite dolls, slingshots, tea sets, and action figures. They remember what was good, sweet, and fun. If you're nearby as they explore that closet, chances are you'll hear some great stories.

That's what we're doing at depth one of *what's stuck*. We're remembering the life-giving nature of our current ruts to affirm what those ruts once provided. When we talk about rutted joys, we're not confessing anything bad; we're reminiscing about something good that ran its course.

A FEW QUESTIONS TO ASK

- What are your most nostalgic habits?
- When you first became a Christian, what habits were most important to you?
- What's the most unique, enjoyable habit you've ever had, and why did you like it?

Chapter 27

WHAT'S STUCK? WHEN THE COLOR BEGAN TO FADE

DEPTH TWO

In our bedroom, we have dried flowers from our wedding in a vase on the dresser. They're still beautiful, but over the last twenty-plus years they've lost some of their color. What was once lavender is drifting toward an ever-duller gray.

That is the fate of all joys and life-giving habits this side of heaven. Yes, God's mercies "are new every morning" (Lamentations 3:23), but our capacity to savor and appreciate them wanes. I remember taking my oldest son on his first big roller-coaster ride. It was a thrill like no other. Through his early teenage years, we rode ever-bigger roller coasters trying to recapture that initial thrill, but we never could.

When life-giving habits fade, it is due to this limited human capacity to savor good things. This is often misunderstood and leads to many life disruptions. How many marriages are discarded because established love is less vibrant than young love? How many life goals die because implementing a dream is less exciting than initially dreaming it?

In depth two of *what's stuck*, we ask what life-giving habits are fading into lifeless ruts. What activities, habits, or relationships were once an emotional net win but are currently a break-even at best?

Honestly answering these questions is the first step toward avoiding a crisis. It's easy to turn a blind eye to the things that make you feel stuck. Being honest with a friend is the best way to make sure you address your lifeless ruts before hardship or crisis finally forces you to confront them.

Let's consider a famous faded-rut passage in the Bible, Revelation 2:4, where Jesus says, "But I have this against you, that you have abandoned the love you had at first." Why did this fading love become such a problem for the church in Ephesus that remedying it required an apocalyptic message from Jesus in his full heavenly glory? Not because it was uncommon or irredeemable, but because it was ignored.

To borrow from a 1990s drunk-driving commercial, friends don't let friends ignore rut problems. Friends ask. Friends listen. Friends appreciate honesty. Friends acknowledge their own ruts. Friends help each other find ways to bring the good in the rut back to life.

The key word for *what's stuck* depth two is *when?*

- Did the rut begin during a **life transition**? Possibly what worked for you in college didn't fit your young-professional or young-family season of life. When life changes, habits often need to be updated.
- Did the stagnation emerge from **too many repetitions**? Perhaps like my approach to Bible reading, you did the same thing the same way too many times and it became stale.
- Did the fade happen as your **values changed**? Maybe after the loss of a friend, what was important to you shifted and you didn't realize how it affected this habit.
- Did the lifelessness develop because a **marker of maturity** didn't? Could it be that your dissatisfaction in marriage is

because your definition of love did not mature as fast as you and your spouse aged?

When is a clue to discerning *why*. Understanding why helps us know how to respond to the fade. In the examples above, fading because of the differences between college and young-professional life requires creative adaptations, but fading because your definition of love is younger than your marriage is a call to maturity.

Have the courage to ask the questions. Allow the support of a friend to ensure the needed change doesn't just become a valid insight lost to good intentions.

A FEW QUESTIONS TO ASK

- What habit used to be "wow" that's now just "eh"?
- What habit fit well in a previous season of life but is hard to find a place for now?
- What makes you sad to realize you don't enjoy it as much as you once did?

Chapter 28

WHAT'S STUCK? WHEN GUILT AND DUTY TOOK OVER

DEPTH THREE

When things that were once life-giving are now drab, we often feel guilty. We wonder, "What's *wrong* with me?" This is how guilt begins to fill our ruts like water on the dirt roads of my old farm. The result is that we mire down and get stuck.

What's the first thing you do with a muddy rut? Drain the ditch. In this metaphor, the water creating the mud is feelings of guilt. If the guilt we feel comes from some sin, some part of *what's bad*, then we should embrace God's gift of repentance. But here I want to explore those times we feel guilty because something that once was life-giving has faded. That's not actually guilt; it's a form of regret or grief.

When we mistake grief for guilt, we motivate ourselves to "do better" with guilt. The worst thing about guilt motivation is that it kind of works, at least for a little while. Guilt motivation is like energizing your body with caffeine and junk food. In the short term, it stimulates change, but there's no nutritional value that comes with it.

Guilt motivation thinks about once-joyful habits like this: *I know I should do ________, so I'll just keep doing it even though it feels lifeless. I must be a bad Christian because I no longer enjoy ________. I don't want anyone to know that ________ doesn't bring me joy anymore, so I just won't talk about it.* These are code-yellow (maybe orange) warnings in your private thought life. They are signals that you need to phone a friend.

When did you start thinking this way about what's stuck? When these kinds of thoughts echo in your mind, what do they sound like? What phrases do you use? How do you beat yourself up?

Guilt motivation compels us with duty rather than sparking creativity. Guilt locks down on *I should* and fails to ask *how could I . . . ?* Let's take a few common examples:

- "*I should* enjoy reading my Bible more," versus, "*How could I* vary my quiet time?"
- "*I should* enjoy my family more," versus, "*How could we* invest in what's meaningful to one another and fits this season of life better?"
- "*I should* enjoy being generous more," versus, "*How could I* be more intentional about seeing the impact of caring for others instead of merely expecting the act of giving to be inherently satisfying?"

With each *I should*, our eyes drop to our feet with guilt. With each *how could*, our eyes scan for possibilities. Recall the imagery David used in Psalm 3:3 when he called out to God in his distress and called him "the lifter of my head."

When we are honest with our friends, they can be the ambassador of God's hand coming gently under our chin to lift our head. They can be the tangible expression of God's tender gaze catching our eyes as our head lifts, reminding us that ruts should not be sources of condemnation but calls to creativity.

A good friend can say: "I appreciate you being honest about how you feel stuck. That takes courage and shows how much you value our friendship. Thank you." A good friend can smile and tell us, "I don't want you to feel stuck. What if we think about how you could . . . ?"

More than the brainstorming session, that question is an invitation to escape the prison of false guilt without dismissing the real concern. This is what Proverbs 27:9 means when it says, "Oil and perfume make the heart glad, and the sweetness of a friend comes from his earnest counsel." When things are stuck, the caring words of a friend can reinvigorate what was good in our ruts, just as a favorite aroma can bring new life to a moment that's gone stale.

A FEW QUESTIONS TO ASK

- When do you feel bad (dry or guilty) about what should make you feel good (edified)?
- What are you doing simply because you know you should?
- What do you dread that you used to be excited about?

Chapter 29
WHAT'S STUCK? HOW YOU'RE STUCK IN STUBBORNNESS
DEPTH FOUR

Sometimes we're blindly stuck, but other times we're willfully stuck. If your response to the past three chapters was, "Oh! That makes sense. How could I not have seen that?" then a little creative brainstorming with a friend is likely all you need to get out of that rut.

But others of us thought, "Grrr! Get off my back. I don't care if it's a lifeless rut, that's just how I do things. Leave me alone." In that case, you're going to need to welcome a friend in at a deeper level for God's next piece of sanctification (positive change toward Christlikeness) to occur.

Since we're talking about stubbornness, let's acknowledge that everything happening or not happening at this level is your choice. Friends don't *force* friends to change. That would be coercion, not influence. Depth four of *what's stuck* is where things can often get sideways between friends. Just because ruts are painfully obvious doesn't mean they're welcome terrain. You'll need humility to welcome friends into these conversations.

What kinds of things might we be talking about here?

- **Parenting:** Maybe the habit of having high goals for your children is becoming the rut of pushing your kids so hard you're pushing them away.
- **Work:** Perhaps the habit of seizing every opportunity has resulted in neglecting family, compromising ethically, or dishonoring competitors in the workplace.
- **Morality:** Possibly the habit of holding to the highest possible standard is pushing you toward being a judgmental, legalistic, and unpleasant person.

In each of these examples, the motive for the rut is good enough that we could argue for its continuance. But the effect of the rut is disruptive. The rut is a good thing that is being emphasized to such a degree that its negative consequences outweigh the good intent. This should remind you of what we said about idols (chapter 17). Remember, worship—pursuing what we want most—is at the center of human motivation. This is why we can expect positive change to push us toward godliness.

The good that motivates our stubborn ruts so easily blinds us to the bad in how we pursue it. That's why we need friends. Friends can see our blind spots.

This is what Jesus warned against in Matthew 23:23, "Woe to you, scribes and Pharisees, hypocrites! For you tithe mint and dill and cumin, and have neglected the weightier matters of the law: justice and mercy and faithfulness. These you ought to have done, without neglecting the others." The Pharisees valued a good thing to the neglect of more important things.

Because of the adversarial relationship between Jesus and the Pharisees, it is easy to miss that Jesus is trying to be a good friend, not a rival, when he says this. Jesus is not being spiteful or cutting. He is giving a truthful warning about a rutted problem.

When our good intentions become rutted, we become as stubborn and prideful as the Pharisees. When this happens, we hear Christlike warnings from friends as if they were attacks from adversaries. We treat a helping hand like a finger pointed in judgment.

At depth four of *what's stuc*k, our call is to give our friends the benefit of the doubt. The trust we've developed as we've moved toward being depth-thirty friends should be the salve that heals our pride-blurred vision. Cooperating with this miracle starts with saying, "That's hard for me to hear, but I trust you have my best interest at heart. Can you walk me into what you're saying a bit more slowly?"

A FEW QUESTIONS TO ASK

- What good thing are you likely to value so much it blinds you to negative consequences?
- What's an example of a time you were convinced you were right but realized you were wrong?
- What's the best way to approach you with something you likely don't want to hear?

Chapter 30

WHAT'S STUCK? HOW YOU'RE STUCK IN SHAME

DEPTH FIVE

When ruts don't crash your life with guilt, they weigh it down with shame. That's why good friends need to be as skilled in applying the gospel to shame as they are in applying it to guilt.

At the deepest levels of each question, we've frequently explored the experience of shame. Shame may be the most isolating emotion. This means friendship is one of the most potent remedies for shame.

With ruts, shame often takes the form of "I shouldn't feel this way." Instead of thinking, "These emotions reveal something is *off*," we think, "These emotions mean something is *wrong with me*." Ruts do reveal that something is off. Good things have become lifeless, mindless, numb, or faded.

God is not angered by ruts, in the same way God is not angered by stale conversations between friends. He wants change, but he's not angry. Ruts don't merit being rejected by others. They don't deserve a sense of self-condemnation. When we feel these things, we are buying into shame's lies.

A primary remedy for being stuck in shame is listening to our unpleasant emotions like a friend who has something valuable to say. This is what David does in Psalm 42:5 when he asks, "Why are you cast down, O my soul, and why are you in turmoil within me?" He can tell something is off, but he isn't ashamed to explore it.

If you read the Psalms, you may be surprised to find that we are much more afraid of our unpleasant emotions than the Bible is. The Bible is far more transparent about life than we are. The Bible is an invitation to greater honesty with ourselves, with God, and with our trusted friends.

Depth five under *what's stuck* invites us to have Psalm 42 types of conversations with our friends. It's when we discuss our answers to questions such as:

- Why are you unresponsive to my quiet time, O my soul?
- Why are you numb to the things that brought me joy for so long, O my soul?
- Why has a sense of purpose evaporated from my job, O my soul?
- Why have conversations with my spouse or friends become rote, O my soul?
- Why has my involvement at church become so flat and routine, O my soul?

When we ask these questions, we're acknowledging that something is off. We're acknowledging that if our lives were flourishing, we wouldn't feel this way. Best of all, we can acknowledge this without avoiding eye contact with our friends. We can acknowledge it with hope.

If you and your friend need more guidance to navigate these conversations than the example of Psalm 42, consider reading *Untangling Emotions* by Alasdair Groves and Winston Smith.[1] It teaches you how to value and listen to emotions, even the unpleasant ones, to grow in your faith and relationships.

---

1. J. Alasdair Groves and Winston T. Smith, *Untangling Emotions* (Wheaton, IL: Crossway, 2019).

This approach is more practical than trying to invert your unpleasant emotions by the force of your will: I am sad, but I *should* be happy, or I am depressed, but I *should* be hopeful. Many of us have become disheartened trying to force ourselves to feel differently.

Instead, when your soul is cast down—when part of your life is stuck, and you feel ashamed because of it—engage in a Psalm 42 conversation with a friend. Refuse to allow isolation to act like a microphone that amplifies your shame. Instead, allow the caring presence of a friend to mute shame as you talk about the rut which prompted it.

A FEW QUESTIONS TO ASK

- What unpleasant emotion do you most often feel that you think you shouldn't feel?
- What are you embarrassed to admit you don't enjoy?
- What's stuck in your life that makes you feel a sense of shame or worthlessness?

Summative Exercise 6

HABIT-BY-HABIT HEAT CHECK

Let's make a color-coded thermometer to indicate how life-giving a habit you practice currently is. Here are the degrees of warmth on this thermometer:

- **Red:** Better than it's ever been!
- **Orange:** Really good
- **Yellow:** Satisfactory
- **Gray:** Fading
- **Blue:** Frozen, an emotional net loss
- **Black:** The habit is absent

With this color-coded indicator in mind, go through the areas of your life where habits emerge.

1. Home and family
2. Work or school
3. Spiritual life, church, or ministry
4. Social life
5. Daily, weekly, and monthly rhythms
6. Recreation, exercise, or health

Once a month, set aside time with a depth-five friend to discuss your habits in one of these six areas. Give them a color and then describe your rationale for that rating. If you do this, you'll assess each major area of habits twice a year.

Another approach for this heat-check exercise is to set aside one prayer time per quarter in your small group to assess how life-giving your habits are in one of these six areas. Embedding this exercise in a small group allows members to get to know the normal of each other's lives better than we often do in a discipleship setting.

If you get a response that is between yellow and black, consider this three-question follow-up:

- **Assess:** How did I get here? What did I like at first? How has life changed since then?
- **Evaluate:** What are new options? What might revitalize the faded habit? Has life changed enough that this habit is obsolete?
- **Decide:** Do I want to do anything different? If so, what?

No, this isn't fancy. But the rhythm of regularly assessing your habits with people you trust is an excellent rut-prevention tactic. Sometimes, a life-changing step is far simpler than we think.

Question 7: What's Next?

Depth One: The Dreams That Got You Here

Depth Two: The Dream You're Working On

Depth Three: The Dream That's Fading

Depth Four: The Dream for the Next Season of Life

Depth Five: The Dream You Are Afraid to Say

Human beings are distinct from animals because we dream. We create goals for the future that produce a sense of anticipation. Squirrels may store nuts for the winter (preparation), but humans dream about things like graduation, marriage, career advancement, and grandchildren (aspiration). We live for *what's next*.

Being made in God's image and redeemed by Jesus means we were made for a purpose, "created in Christ Jesus for good works" (Ephesians 2:10). The human reflex to dream and set goals is evidence that God made each of us for a reason. Ultimately, that reason is to know and enjoy God forever. For each one of us personally, that reason matches up with the unique talents and passions God gave us.

Friendship between Christians is what happens as our dreams run in parallel. We pursue the things God made us to do. We notice and build relationships with those around us. These emerging friendships are part of God's design to compel and encourage us along that journey.

Dreams also give life meaning. Dreams are the connective tissue between the seemingly mundane activities of day-to-day life. Career aspirations make the hundreds of school assignments worth it. Athletic goals give meaning to each repetition in the weight room. Desire for friendship motivates us to perform the daily sacrifices that show people we care.

A life without dreams is meaningless. Without dreams, even good deeds feel like mere busywork to keep us constructively occupied.

But dreams without friendship die the death of good intentions. If you have a goal and speak of it to no one, what usually happens? A little enthusiasm followed by nothing.

But if you have a dream and share it with a friend, what happens? Your ongoing conversations will generate shared enthusiasm, brainstorming, prayer, and incremental follow-through.

That's the *what's next* journey: sharing your goals and dreams so that you and your friends become mutually encouraging companions on the hard-but-enjoyable journey of fulfilling as many of your dreams as possible. Let's go!

Chapter 31

WHAT'S NEXT? THE DREAMS THAT GOT YOU HERE

DEPTH ONE

Yesterday's dreams have a propensity for becoming today's assumptions. Yesterday we had an aspiration. It seemed challenging, far off. We worked hard, prayed, enlisted support, and the dream became a reality. From that new height, we looked up, identified a new dream, and aspired again. If we're not careful, yesterday's dreams simply become the floor from which we jump toward our next set of goals.

Friendship can be a wonderful speed bump to disrupt taking yesterday's answered prayers for granted. Conversations about the dreams that got you here are a great way to resuscitate the encouragement from yesterday's answered prayers. As you talk about these dreams, discuss the angst before the dream was realized, the drive it required to accomplish that goal, and the enthusiasm when doubt gave way to fulfillment.

Exercise: Tell your life story by moving from one dream to the next. We usually tell our story by moving through life stages (childhood, middle school, high school, etc.) or places we've lived. But try telling your story using the major goals and dreams that motivated you.

Think of this as the Tarzan version of your story. Tarzan swung across the jungle from one vine to the next. We move through life swinging from one dream to the next. Telling the goal-to-goal, dream-to-dream version of your story is a great way to build rapport in a friendship as you each get excited about the things that compelled you to this point in your life.

Don't leave out the dreams that didn't get fulfilled. Those dreams still count. Those dreams still shape you, often in positive ways. Unfulfilled dreams aren't wasted. They're usually just useful in ways we didn't anticipate. They shape character, form skills, or build resilience.

As you share your dreams, give yourself the freedom to be amused by the innocence and frivolity of early dreams. Have the courage to thank God for prayers that were best unanswered. Allow yourself to get excited again as you talk about goals achieved. This full-spectrum authenticity as you share is what forges a bond of feeling known by a new friend.

If you need a primer for this kind of exercise, trace the dreams that we can imagine marked each stage of Moses's life.

- Early in life, Moses wanted to be safe and free (Exodus 2).
- In school, Moses wanted to be top of the class (Acts 7:22).
- After graduation, Moses wanted revenge (Exodus 2:11–15).
- Then Moses wanted a life unmarred by regret (Exodus 2:16–22).
- After the burning bush, Moses wanted freedom for others (Exodus 3–15).
- After the Red Sea parted, Moses just wanted the people to stop grumbling (Exodus 16).
- After being a leader for a while, Moses wanted relief from his work (Exodus 18).

Tell your story dream-to-dream, prayer-to-prayer, goal-to-goal, burden-to-burden, passion-to-passion. Listen to yourself tell of God's faithfulness. Listen to this version of your story like music from your teenage years. For me, that's 90s country music. I hear it and it feels like home. It takes me back, in vivid ways, to memories that would otherwise be lost.

Be moved afresh by examples of God's faithfulness that you haven't thought about in a long time. Share these memories, dreams, and accompanying emotions with a friend. It will lay a foundation for your friendship that can become a beautiful source of encouragement.

A FEW QUESTIONS TO ASK

- Tell me your story one life dream at a time.
- What was the most satisfying goal you've accomplished?
- What have you had to work hardest to achieve in your life?

Chapter 32

WHAT'S NEXT? THE DREAM YOU'RE WORKING ON

DEPTH TWO

Past dreams build hope for current dreams. Depth one of *what's next* lays the foundation for depth two, the dream you're working on now. Talking about past dreams gives us an emotional running start in the pursuit of current dreams.

A theme verse for depth-two friendship under *what's next* is Hebrews 10:24, "Let us consider how to stir up one another to love and good works." At this depth, we're learning the specific good works God has laid on the heart of our friend, so we can spur them on toward those dreams.

Oddly, it may catch us by surprise how mundane many of these goals are. A word like *dream* seems like it should always sparkle, but some of life's most meaningful dreams are a bit dingy.

- Being a person of integrity looks like having hard conversations, not cutting corners.
- Being a good parent looks like responding to daily dramas, even the silly ones, with care.

- Retiring with means to pursue other dreams looks like saying no to lots of little things for decades to put yourself in the position to say yes to a few big things.
- Even something as grand as being a world-class athlete involves lots of mundane practice, weight training, nutrition, and film study.

The most satisfying dreams aren't achieved in epic moments but through daily faithfulness in moments that are easy to miss. A life of godly character infuses these ordinary moments with uncanny significance. Friendship is pivotal to persevering in the mundane journey that results in these extraordinary moments.

Exercise: Go through the various areas of your life and articulate the goals you want to work toward.

- Health
- Relationships
- Occupation and finances
- Spiritual life, ministry opportunities, and character
- Recreation and hobbies

Do the people you call friends know these goals? If not, that's like hiring a personal chef but withholding the types of food you enjoy. It's like hiring a taxi but not providing the destination. Friends who don't know our dreams lose all their "stir up one another to love and good works" power.

Without mutual awareness of each other's dreams, friends "just hang out." Knowing each other's dreams gives friendship a sense of direction. Hanging out can be fun, especially when we need to recuperate. But if our friendships are going to be more than an oasis on the side of life, our friends need to know our current dreams.

A FEW QUESTIONS TO ASK

- What dream or goal can I be praying about for you?
- What's the most important thing I can encourage you toward in this season of life?
- What important thing is easiest for you to neglect?

Chapter 33

WHAT'S NEXT? THE DREAM THAT'S FADING

DEPTH THREE

Dreams have expiration dates, and we're all getting older. A few of our life dreams may be evergreens, but most of them will be like the leaves on mountain trees in the fall. That is part of life as finite creatures in a transient world.

Our theme verse for depth three under *what's next* is Romans 12:15: "Rejoice with those who rejoice, weep with those who weep." The weeping part is our focus. Deepening friendships grieve fading dreams.

Ironically, I began writing the first draft of this chapter on my oldest son's eighteenth birthday. It is a fitting marker for what this chapter is all about. Lots of dreams are reaching their conclusion as he and I think about college, career, and his next season of life.

It has been an amazing eighteen years that have enriched my life in more ways than words can express, even for a guy who writes for a living. There is much to celebrate. But whatever will be done has been done. The years before he became an adult have been spent. Whatever has not been done will not be done. Once I've learned what I can learn about priorities, there is no value in wading further through the swamp of regret or nostalgia.

What dreams are fading for you? What life markers were once in front of you but are now (or soon will be) behind you? Where is the undefeated champion, Father Time, claiming a victory in your life? What once-promising and fulfilling dream is it now time to grieve?

As you ponder these different ways of asking the same question, you and your friend should reinforce at least three points in each other's lives.

First, it takes courage to acknowledge dreams that didn't get fulfilled, or at least that the time to enjoy that dream has passed. It is cowardice or childish fantasy to pretend otherwise. Affirm the courage in your friend as you talk.

Second, maturity is defined by knowing when to let dreams transition. Much of immaturity is clinging to expired dreams. You know the people who are still living as if high school or college were the greatest years of their life. Affirm the maturity of releasing faded dreams to embrace new ones.

Third, don't mistake unfulfilled dreams for failure. I wanted to be a professional baseball player, and I learned a work ethic by chasing that dream. I wanted to be a computer programmer, and I learned to accept my limitations more humbly after Calculus 1. Unfulfilled dreams can have a multitude of residual blessings.

As you grieve fading dreams together, you are going through a kind of friendship rite of passage. I had a college friend named David who was a fellow baseball walk-on. We had many conversations after practice as we each realized our life stories weren't going to be the baseball version of the movie *Rudy*. Going through that grief-maturation process forges a bond. It takes friendship to a new depth.

These life markers are going to happen whether you allow them to forge a friendship or not. One of the ways you redeem these transitions is by allowing them to become rites of passage for your friendships. As you grieve with your friend who grieves, you are serving as a companion from one season of life to the next, from one dream pursuit to another. Even with its tinge of sadness, that's special.

A FEW QUESTIONS TO ASK

- What was the hardest dream for you to relinquish?
- What dream do you sense is coming to a close?
- How will your goals change in the next season of life?

Chapter 34

WHAT'S NEXT? THE DREAM FOR THE NEXT SEASON OF LIFE

DEPTH FOUR

Depth three under *what's next* was about grief for what we've lost, but depth four is about anticipation of what we might gain. Like in a series such as *The Chronicles of Narnia* or *Star Wars*, these are the points in our life when one book ends and the next begins. As you move from one book to the next in these series, most of the setting and culture are the same but a new plot is emerging. The new plot demands new goals. There are new challenges to meet.

In one *Star Wars* movie, a Jedi destroys the Death Star. In the next *Star Wars* movie, a descendant of that Jedi destroys another planet-munching machine (I know I didn't get it exactly right). In one *Narnia* book, four children from our world defeat the White Witch. In another *Narnia* book, two of those children rescue a trapped prince with the help of their old talking animal friends.

In *what's next* depth four, we're recognizing that each season of our life is a sequel to the one before, with most of the same characters but new points of angst that require new goals and dreams. (You can decide who in your life is a Wookiee and who is Puddleglum.)

Let's stick with the *Narnia* series to develop this metaphor. What happens each time the children from this world get pulled into Narnia? They are disoriented because Narnia has changed. What happens when we transition from one season of life to the next? We get disoriented because, while most of the characters and terrain are the same, important things have changed.

We must gain our bearings. Identifying new goals and dreams is an essential part of gaining our bearings in each new season of life.

- As we move from high school to college, how do we pursue goals without the regulatory oversight of our parents?
- As we move from college to career, how do we define goals without the assistance of a syllabus?
- As we move from single to married life, how are goals formed as a *we* instead of a *me*?
- When children become part of our life, how does having dependents impact goal formation?
- When children reach the point of having their own life ambitions, how do we navigate the divergence of their dreams and ours?
- When retirement sneaks up on us, how do we create goals when life is shorter than it's ever been?

Each season of life brings its own angst that calls for different dreams and goals. The friends that bridge these seasons of life become endearing characters in our life like C-3PO or the faun, Tumnus. Inviting friends into these transitions helps us and our friend recognize the changes that are happening.

What's next depth four is Philippians 3:13 in action, "forgetting what lies behind and straining forward to what lies ahead." You and your friend are not erasing memories of the past, but you are fully giving yourselves to the dreams and goals of this season of life. You are straining toward the resolution of present challenges rather than being distracted by expired dreams.

As you bridge seasons of life, have intentional conversations with your friends. This maximizes how much you learn from the past, and it sets you up to live fully in the present chapter of your life. As too many of us have learned the hard way, this doesn't happen by accident. Grow your friendships by acknowledging, exploring, and embracing the new seasons of life together.

A FEW QUESTIONS TO ASK

- What is least clear to you about your present season of life?
- What goals are possible now that weren't viable in previous seasons of life?
- What goals did you use to think you would have for this season of life, and how is this season different from what you imagined?

Chapter 35

WHAT'S NEXT? THE DREAM YOU ARE AFRAID TO SAY

DEPTH FIVE

With all seven questions, we've sought to keep reaching greater depths of vulnerability. This is not because we're trying to recreate the emotional–relational angst of skydiving, but because friendships that change our lives are friendships with people who truly know us. *What's next* is no different. With that in mind, let's explore the dreams you are afraid to tell anyone about.

You might mistake the answer for your unorthodox bucket-list ideas: "I want to rappel down a waterfall at sunset and be engulfed in a rainbow before I die." That's not what we're talking about.

These are the dreams that feel too big to speak. Maybe you've always wanted to get a PhD. Perhaps you want to retire on the mission field. Possibly you have a business idea you've wanted to launch.

Here's the thing: unspoken dreams don't come true. Spoken dreams may or may not come true, but unspoken dreams die the death of silence. Speaking a dream to a friend is the first step toward finding out if it's possible. If it is possible, we may or may not decide the necessary sacrifices are worth it. But silence archives any dream.

Why don't we share these dreams? We don't want to sound stupid. We don't want to put a big dream out there and then fail.

Why have you done five levels of work on seven questions? In part, to get over the fear of rejection and failure. To establish friendships that are an accelerator, not an obstacle, to becoming the person God created you to be. You honor and affirm your depth-thirty-plus friends by trusting them with these dreams.

Speaking a dream doesn't commit you to anything. It does allow people to pray for you. It allows you to get more information and to vet possibilities. But more than that, it allows you to be known at a deeper level. Even if nothing comes of the dream, your friendships will be closer.

We see an example of this in Paul. In Romans 1:13, Paul shares, "I do not want you to be unaware, brothers, that I have often intended to come to you." Ministering in Rome was Paul's dream. Undoubtedly, he talked about it often. But each time he thought it might happen, something came up. By the time he wrote his letter to the Romans, he still hadn't been there. But at the end in chapter 16, we see he has a full chapter's worth of friends in Rome whom he greets. His friends had fulfilled Paul's dream in his stead.

This isn't primarily a goal-fulfillment book. It's a friendship book. *In friendship, we must take the risk of being known if we are going to know the joy of being loved*. Sharing the dreams that feel too big, too far off, or too much out of our comfort zone is how we do that with *what's next*.

Here's my own depth-five *what's next* answer: I want to see thousands upon thousands of Christians begin to experience within the church friendships that will transform their lives. I want the biblical idea of church as family to be more than a metaphor. I want the quality of friendships within the church to become so attractive to a relationally starved culture that it becomes a prompt for a fresh movement of people coming to faith in Christ and being discipled well.

That's a big dream. It feels awkward and intimidating to put it in print. But like any big dream, it can only be realized if it's spoken and then implemented in a series of mundane moments. In this case, that's you and your friends growing deeper in your friendships—one question at a time.

A FEW QUESTIONS TO ASK

- What dream are you too intimidated or self-conscious about to share?
- What goal do you have that feels too far off to say?
- If you weren't worried about failing, what would you try to do?

Summative Exercise 7

PRAYING FOR YOUR FRIEND'S DREAMS LIKE YOUR OWN

What's one of the truest markers of an excellent friend? They pray for your dreams as fervently as they pray for their own. They get as excited about your progress toward your dreams as their progress toward their dreams.

There are a variety of ways you can do this as a friend. Consider the following:

- When your friend shares a dream or goal, write it down. Put it wherever you keep up with prayer items. Text your friend when you pray for it.
- Let your friend know when their dream comes to mind. My son currently wants to become a pilot, so I text him a picture of things I see that are aviation related.
- In your small group, play a goal-focused version of Secret Santa. Ask each person to write down their name and a current dream/goal. Put the pieces of paper in a bowl and have each person select one. For the person whose name and goal you drew, spend a month looking for ways to anonymously encourage them toward their dream. After a month, invite each person to share their dream and an update on the progress, and then reveal who their secret encourager was.

Here's the essence of what you're communicating: *I'm on your team*. Teammates have shared dreams even if they have different roles. Friends share each other's goals even if they are pursuing different dreams.

For example, a twenty-year-old college student can get excited with her forty-year-old mentor, who is hosting a discipleship event for her high school son's youth group. The student can pray for a fruitful weekend and ask how it went. And that mentor can get excited about the college student's applications to grad school. The mentor can pray for guidance amid the options and celebrate the acceptance letter. We can be on each other's teams even as we pursue different dreams in different seasons of life.

So, here's another way to ask the same question: Do your friends know you wear their jerseys? When you're invested in the success of a team, you wear their apparel. Metaphorically speaking, who knows you're wearing a hat with their logo? You can let them know in the following ways:

- Remembering important dates related to their goals and dreams. Encourage before and follow up afterward. When a friend realizes you're keeping up with their important dates, they know you're on their team.
- Learning the language related to their goals and dreams. Most goals have verbiage you learn when you pursue them. When someone hears you use the language of their dream, they know you're on their team.
- Expressing availability. Say something like, "I'm excited about ______. Please, let me know how I can support you in pursuing it."

Consider these ideas brainstorming prompts. If these possibilities don't sound like you, ask yourself, *How would I communicate to someone that I am as excited about their dreams as I am about my own? How would I let them know I'm on their team?*

CLOSING THOUGHTS

With the friendship questions now in your hands, I have a few closing thoughts for you as you step out to use them. The first is this: *don't paint by numbers; play jazz*.

Do you remember the coloring books where each segment of the picture had a number in it and there was a key to tell you what color corresponds with each number? As long as you followed the instructions, you were guaranteed to create a work of art that wouldn't embarrass your mother to put on the refrigerator. This book is not like that, as tempting as it may be to use it that way.

This book is not a *recipe* for meaningful relationships. Instead, it's a *melody* for friendships that can transform your life.

As musically inept as I am, I know a bit about jazz. With jazz, there is no sheet music, no lined chart with notes for each musician to follow. Instead, each musician riffs off the melody and adapts to the other musicians in the band. That's what makes jazz feel more alive than other styles of music. Even the same song, played by the same musicians, is different each time.

Your friendships will flourish the most if you treat these seven questions like the melody for a jazz band rather than the key in a numbered coloring book. Yes, the goal is to go deeper in your relational intentionality—but to do that without creating a formula to follow, routines that become stale, or robotic checklists. Friendship must be more alive than that.

To play relational jazz, you should understand the big picture behind our questions. You need a sense of the forest after we've marked the trees. So, let's contrast how each question provides an opportunity to differentiate *transformative friendships* from *stagnant friendships*.

1. **What's your story?** Transformative friends **know** each other, so as the friendship ages, the knowing intentionally deepens. Stagnant friends merely absorb time in each other's lives in mutually enjoyable ways.
2. **What's good?** Transformative friends **affirm** the good gifts from God in each other's lives because they want to contribute to seeing their friend flourish. Stagnant friends treat these good qualities like background music in a restaurant that occasionally gets a passing comment.
3. **What's hard?** Transformative friends **support** each other in hard times and remind each other that *hard* (suffering) doesn't mean *bad* (sin). Stagnant friends prefer to steer clear of the discomfort that comes with meaningfully engaging hard times.
4. **What's bad?** Transformative friends **engage** as allies in each other's battle against the inherent human selfishness that would devour our lives. Stagnant friends fear being perceived as judgmental, so they avoid these uncomfortable topics.
5. **What's fun?** Transformative friends **delight** in the joy of their friends and seek to enhance their joy. Stagnant friends depend solely upon common interests and convenient engagements to make the relationship emotionally "worth it."
6. **What's stuck?** Transformative friends **assess** life together and make sure old habits are still serving current dreams. Stagnant friends let life happen until a crisis jolts us out of our ruts.
7. **What's next?** Transformative friends **pursue** each other's dreams by praying for and investing in those dreams coming to fruition. Stagnant friends merely click "like" on a social media post when something good happens in each other's lives.

This is the melody: (1) know, (2) affirm, (3) support, (4) engage, (5) delight, (6) assess, and (7) pursue. Riff on that melody. Each depth of the growing roots is merely a way to determine "Where are we?" and a brainstorming prompt for "Where could we take our friendship from here?" Be creative and allow each friendship to develop a life of its own within this melody. Play relational jazz!

FRIENDSHIP ASSESSMENT

Some of us have that friend, and others of us *are* that friend for whom a visual tool makes all the difference in implementing a new concept. Never fear: if that's you, here you go. Use the one-page assessment on the next page, based on our roots metaphor for the seven questions, as you look for ways to go deeper in your friendships. You can download a full-sized version at bradhambrick.com/FriendshipRoots. The instructions are simple.

1. Use one copy of this assessment for each of your meaningful friendships.
2. Mark where each friendship is on each of the seven questions. You'll notice the five markers from each of the seven questions we've explored.
3. For **specific friendships**: First, set your expectations for each friendship based on where it *currently* resides and enjoy it at that depth! Then, look for opportunities to intentionally deepen a few friendships. It would be overwhelming to deepen every friendship at the same time.
4. For your **pool of friendships**: First, assess which of the seven questions your pool of friendships tends to neglect. For a variety of reasons, some of our lives are geared more toward certain questions. Then, be intentional to grow deeper in one or more friendships, using those neglected questions.
5. Enjoy life, love your friends, and bring glory to God as you do! *Don't get so caught up in growing that you neglect enjoying.*

SEVEN-QUESTION DEPTH OF FRIENDSHIP ASSESSMENT

Friend: ____

What's Your Story?
- ☐ The Facts
- ☐ The Major Themes
- ☐ The Plot Twists
- ☐ The Life-Shaping Events
- ☐ The Point of Your Story

What's Good?
- ☐ Your Talents
- ☐ Your Quirks
- ☐ Your Roles
- ☐ Your Sacrifices
- ☐ Your Character

What's Hard?
- ☐ The Flip Side of Your Strengths
- ☐ Your Current Life Challenges
- ☐ The Fall Around You
- ☐ The Fall Within You
- ☐ What You've Never Told Anyone

What's Bad?
- ☐ Your Respectable Sins
- ☐ Your Most Prevalent Idols
- ☐ Your Go-To Escapes
- ☐ Your Code-Orange Sins
- ☐ Most Likely to Shipwreck Your Life

What's Fun?
- ☐ What Brings You Joy
- ☐ Why You Enjoy These Things
- ☐ Can I Try It Too?
- ☐ Sacrificing for Your Joys
- ☐ Feeling Your Joys

What's Stuck?
- ☐ When Your Ruts Were Life-Giving
- ☐ When the Color Began to Fade
- ☐ When Guilt and Duty Took Over
- ☐ How You're Stuck in Stubbornness
- ☐ How You're Stuck in Shame

What's Next?
- ☐ The Dreams That Got You Here
- ☐ The Dream You're Working On
- ☐ The Dream That's Fading
- ☐ The Dream for the Next Season of Life
- ☐ The Dream You Are Afraid to Say

If you want to enhance your friendships further, I recommend three books from two of my friends. Jonathan Holmes (yeah, the guy with the daughters from chapter 23) wrote *The Company We Keep: In Search of Biblical Friendship*, which provides a robust theology of friendship. Ed Welch wrote *Caring for One Another: 8 Ways to Cultivate Meaningful Relationships* and *Side by Side: Walking with One Another in Wisdom and Love* to give you more skills for being an effective friend.[1]

Friendship is worth it. Few things change your life more than your friends. You'll never regret investing in increasing the quality of your friendships. Keep going!

YOU DON'T KNOW ME

Don't take offense, but we're not friends. Even after a whole book, you simply know a lot *about* me. I'm familiar to you and, hopefully, as you've heard pieces of my story, I have become someone you trust and respect. But knowing a lot about me doesn't make us friends.

There are people in your life who need you to hear me say this—people like your pastor, perhaps your small group leader, or others who influence your life through one-way communication like preaching and teaching. You know a lot about them. You trust and respect them. They are familiar and endearing to you. But unless your relationship with them meets the two criteria below, your relationship with them is something other than friendship.

First, friendships are marked by *proportional, voluntary knowledge* of each other. When you know me more than I know you (or vice versa), either the friendship is imbalanced or it's a helping relationship being called by the wrong name. Helping

1. Jonathan Holmes *The Company We Keep: In Search of Biblical Friendship* (Minneapolis: Cruciform Press, 2014); Ed Welch, *Caring for One Another: 8 Ways to Cultivate Meaningful Relationships* (Wheaton, IL: Crossway, 2018); Ed Welch, *Side by Side: Walking with One Another in Wisdom and Love* (Wheaton, IL: Crossway, 2015).

relationships like counseling, shepherding, and mentoring are wonderful. But they're not friendships.

Use weightlifting as a visual parallel. Avoid having friendships where the level of mutual awareness is as imbalanced as "that guy" at the gym with a bull chest and chicken legs (if that's you, quit skipping leg day). Build your friendships proportionally.

Why does bull-chicken man work out that way? He has favorite exercises and muscle groups. Why do we develop bull-chicken friendships? We have a favorite area of friendship, and so we focus disproportionately on that question. Or we want to *be* a friend more than we want to *have* a friend. It is safer and less vulnerable to just know and care for others, so we listen more than we share. Conversely, maybe we want to *have* friends more than *be* a friend, so we talk more than we listen.

My goal with the bull-chicken man metaphor is to ensure you won't be able to unsee it. I want the image to be sticky enough that you won't excuse whatever motivates you toward disproportional awareness in your friendships.

Second, friendships are marked by *proportional, shared investment* in the relationship. The first point was about *information*; this point is about *involvement*. Friends have comparable awareness of each other and put comparable effort into their friendship. This doesn't mean everything has to be fifty–fifty, but if it's consistently eighty–twenty it's not a friendship; it's a helping relationship.

You can't force a relationship to be fifty–fifty or sixty–forty. One person's overdoing doesn't mean the other person owes comparable investment in the relationship. That's transactional. It's an unhealthy expectation—in other words, a demand. Friendship is voluntary.

One person wanting more from a friendship than the other has caused many depth-fifteen friendships to reach a hurtful demise. If we're not careful, this book could exacerbate that. Growing deeper in a friendship must be *mutually desired* and *mutually engaged*. It cannot be compelled.

When you want to grow a friendship, be overt about it and take the steps initially to put in the "sixty" portion of a sixty–forty relationship. This book gives you tools to do so. It helps you try not to jump from depth fifteen to depth thirty. But if your efforts are not reciprocated, it is best to enjoy a depth-fifteen friendship with that person and seek someone else to grow a deeper friendship with.

Remember, we've said that all your friendships shouldn't be depth-thirty-five friendships. It's not viable. Your finite time and energy won't allow for it. Part of what you've gained from this book is a tool to determine when a friendship has stalled out at as deep a level as the other person desires. Even if this is disappointing to you, awareness of it is good. It allows you to invest in friendships where there is more openness to deepening that relationship.

TRANSFORMATIVE FRIENDSHIPS AND NON-CHRISTIANS

Repeat after me: "My non-Christian friends are not projects." Too often, the good Christian desire to be evangelistic can make friendships with non-Christians awkward. We should want to be evangelistic. It is right to care about the souls of our non-Christian friends. But our non-Christian friends shouldn't feel like we are their friends just to convert them.

By the way, if you are not a Christian and reading this book, thank you! I appreciate your trust and interest. I hope reflecting on friendship from a Christian perspective has enriched your life. I also hope that reflecting on these seven questions—your story, goodness, suffering, sin, joy, habit, and purpose—has sparked an interest in exploring Christianity further.

Each of these seven questions has natural segues to the gospel that should emerge as our friendships deepen. With our Christian friends, these gospel segues should transform our lives through what is called discipleship. With our non-Christian friends, these segues are opportunities to introduce the gospel.

1. **What's your story?** Human beings seek to make meaning of our lives. We "story" our lives. Knowing your friends' stories gives you a sense of how the gospel would give new meaning to their life (in addition to being incredibly interesting).
2. **What's good?** Rocks and goats don't sin. They don't share the same image-of-God goodness as humans, so that goodness can't be marred in goats like it can in humans. Affirming goodness helps your friend begin to see why sin matters (in addition to being encouraging).
3. **What's hard?** Too many people mistake grief (suffering) for guilt (sin). We are not just ambassadors of God's grace toward sin but also God's comfort amid suffering. Caring well as friends demonstrates that God is more approachable than many people fear.
4. **What's bad?** We are sinners. From day one, no one had to teach us to be selfish. Friends don't ignore sin. Instead of saying, "That's okay," we can acknowledge, "That's not good, but we have a mutual hope in Christ." This is when the gospel comes forth most clearly in a friendship.
5. **What's fun?** God created us to enjoy life. Joy is a fruit of the Spirit, and God is a God of joy (Nehemiah 8:10). Without this emphasis, the gospel becomes as appealing as buying nursing home insurance.
6. **What's stuck?** Good actions begin to have a diminishing emotional return. Those who think being a Christian is merely being a good person can easily mistake this to mean Christianity isn't for them. Understanding the gospel helps differentiate being a Christian from doing more good things than bad things.
7. **What's next?** We all have an innate sense that there ought to be more to this life than daily subsistence. In the absence of a moral crisis (*what's bad*), this question is the second most frequent entry point to overt conversations about the gospel.

Again, repeat after me: "My non-Christian friends are not projects." Intentionality shouldn't lead to poor relational skills. Yes, be intentional. Don't be obnoxious. Yes, look for these segues to the gospel. But also genuinely enjoy the friendship in the times between when these segues emerge.

You might be asking, "What does it sound like to transition from one of these seven questions to the gospel?" It sounds like sharing your life in a way that communicates why the gospel is so important to you.

As Christians, we shouldn't be able to answer these seven questions, especially at the deeper levels, without talking about our faith. When your friend talks about things that are most important to them, you listen with interest. The reverse is true as well. Be a great friend: engage all seven questions together and convey the relevance of the gospel as you do.

Be intentional about deepening your friendships with non-Christians in the same way you are with fellow believers. As the friendship deepens, talk more openly, more passionately, and more vulnerably about your faith. If you do that, you will not only share your faith *frequently*, but you will do so *effectively*.

Appendix
NEW TESTAMENT ONE-ANOTHER PASSAGES

Here is a list of thirty-nine New Testament passages that give commands about how believers are to engage with one another. Okay, I'll admit it. I left out the "greet one another with a holy kiss" passages . . . well . . . because . . . awkward. A handshake or fist bump will suffice in our culture. If you're really close friends, give them a hug.

What should you do with this list? As you read this book, study one passage a day in your personal quiet time. Read the full chapter in which each verse is found. Get the context for each verb that captures biblical friendship.

Allow your quiet time and reading this book to play in concert with one another. Your quiet time provides the *timeless foundation* for biblical friendship. This book provides *timely and descriptive applications* of what it looks like to live out these commands.

Appendix: New Testament One-Another Passages

Mark 9:50
John 13:14
John 13:34–35
John 15:12–17
Romans 12:10
Romans 12:16
Romans 13:8
Romans 14:13
Romans 15:7
Romans 15:14
1 Corinthians 11:33
1 Corinthians 12:25
Galatians 5:13–15
Galatians 5:26
Galatians 6:2
Ephesians 4:2
Ephesians 4:32
Ephesians 5:19
Ephesians 5:21
Philippians 2:3
Colossians 3:9
Colossians 3:13
Colossians 3:16
1 Thessalonians 3:12
1 Thessalonians 4:9
1 Thessalonians 4:18
1 Thessalonians 5:11
Hebrews 3:13
Hebrews 10:24–25
James 4:11
James 5:9
James 5:16
1 Peter 3:8
1 Peter 4:8–10
1 Peter 5:5
1 John 3:11
1 John 3:23
1 John 4:7–12
2 John 5